BOB CHURCH's GUIDE *to* NEW FLY PATTERNS

The Crowood Press

First published in 1993 by
The Crowood Press Ltd
Ramsbury, Marlborough
Wiltshire SN8 2HR

Paperback edition 1999

British Library Cataloguing-in-Publication Data

A catalogue record for this book is available from the British Library.

ISBN 1 86126 306 6

Picture credits:
All illustrations by Peter Gathercole.

Typeset by Footnote Graphics, Warminster, Wiltshire
Printed and bound in China by Leo Paper Products

Contents

Acknowledgements

My special thanks go to all the guest contributors who have given this book so much more variety and interest than it might otherwise have had: to professional tyers such as Davy Wotton, Oliver Edwards, Glynn Hopper, Sid Knight, Micky Bewick and the multi-talented Charles Jardine; to those champion fly-fishers who regularly win competitions with their creations—Svoboda, from Czechoslovakia, Chris Ogborne, from Bristol, rising young star Jeremy Herrmann, from Market Harborough, and Peter Cockwill, the champion of the small fisheries; to Paul Vekemans, from Belgium, Thomas Tykosson, from Sweden, Alun Jenkins, from Wales, Barry Unwin and Peter Dobbs for their special selections from home and abroad.

Finally, special thanks are due also to Jeanette Taylor, who not only typed the final script but contributes as a top fly-tyer; to Peter Gathercole, our finest angling photographer, for his pictures and his own selection; and to John Wilshaw, editor of *Practical Gamefishing*, for his foreword.

Bob Church
1993

Trout fishing without frontiers

Fishing for trout in faraway places
Amid a host of friendly faces.
World Championships in the best traditions,
New Zealand and Spain just two expeditions.
Making good friends, learning from others,
Fishing mates, fishing brothers.
Trout remembered as the best,
Whether from reservoir, lough or exclusive Test.

Bob Church

FOREWORD

We've all tied the infallible fly, that inspired flickering together of fur and feather, only to discover it to be just another nine day wonder that failed after a brief moment of quicksilver fame.

Yet these sad rejects often hold the germ of something really new and exciting, needing just a touch more development or input from other free-thinking fly dressers to make them blossom into flies that will truly stand the test of time.

Wearing his considerable and well deserved reputation lightly, Bob is one of very few top-flight fishers who has retained the common touch, ever ready to lay down his own rod to help a less proficient angler. I fished my first reservoir with Bob twenty years (and a lot of flies lost in the bushes) ago so I know just how invaluable this down-to-earth advice can be and I thank him for it on behalf of all those other newcomers to the sport.

With several standard patterns to his own credit, Bob has, happily for us, a compulsion to peek into other anglers' fly boxes. A few of these patterns, gleaned from fly fishers from America, Australasia and Europe as well as at home, have already trickled into our own fly wallets, but this is the first time that we have been allowed to take a lingering look into this truly international Aladdin's Cave of new flies.

JOHN WILSHAW
Editor, *Practical Gamefishing*

HOW TO TIE A FLY

The only traditional fly in this book is seen in this photographic stage-by-stage tying of the famous Dunkeld wet fly. Experienced fly-tyers may give the pictures only a passing glance, but they are important for beginners and improvers. The sequence shows in detail all the disciplines really needed to tie a good fly. Practise and master this one and you should be ready to tackle any pattern. The principle stays much the same. The changes are in the materials.

This book contains 400 different patterns, all with guidelines on materials and fishing technique. If you have technical problems with your fly-tying, remember that almost certainly a club or evening classes will be available not too far away where you will be welcome. Meanwhile, enjoy the challenge that these patterns bring.

Dunkeld

(1) Fix a standard round-bend wet-fly hook in the vice and run on black pre-waxed tying thread from the eye.
(2) Carry the thread down the shank to a point opposite the barb. Select a well-coloured golden pheasant crest feather and catch it in as a tail at the bend.
(3) Take three inches of fine gold tinsel, which will later form the rib, and catch it in at the same point as the tail. Then take the tying thread up towards the eye in neat, touching turns.
(4) Take three inches of medium-width gold Lurex and cut one end to a point, which will help in winding the initial turns and prevent bulk forming at the eye.
(5) Catch in the Lurex by the point, just behind the eye, and wind it down to the tail in closely butted turns with no gaps. That done, wind the tinsel back to its catching-in point.

(6) The double layer of Lurex gives a very smooth effect. Secure the waste end.
(7) Now select a dyed-orange cock hackle with fibres about one-and-a-half times the hook-gape. Remove the fluffy waste from the hackle's base to leave a section of bare hackle stalk. Trim this to a short stub and use this to catch-in the hackle securely just behind the eye.
(8) Take hold of the tip with a pair of hackle pliers and wind the hackle down towards the tail in a neat, open spiral. Five or six turns are ample.
(9) Keeping tension on the wound hackle, take hold of the gold tinsel and begin winding it up towards the eye. It should be wound so that each turn of tinsel traps a turn of hackle.
(10) Secure the loose end of rib, trim off the excess, and tease out any hackle-fibres which have become trapped.
(11) That accomplished, select and remove a slip of bronze mallard three times the width of the intended wing, so that when one edge is folded to the centre and then over again, it forms a rolled wing ready to be tied in.
(12) Judge the wing-slip for length. Personal preference has much to do with this decision though one-and-a-quarter to one-and-a-half times the length of the hook-shank is a general guide.
(13) Once the wing has been secured with two or three winging loops plus extra turns of thread, remove the excess butts flush with the eye with a pair of sharp scissors.
(14) Select a pair of small, well-coloured jungle-cock feathers or substitute and remove the fluffy material from the base of each.
(15) Secure one on either side of the wing, making sure that they are the same length.
(16) To complete the Dunkeld, remove the stubs of jungle-cock feather, build a small, neat head, finish it off with the mandatory five-turn whip-finish and give a coat of varnish to the bare threads.

There you have it: a well-tied Dunkeld, and the key to most other patterns.

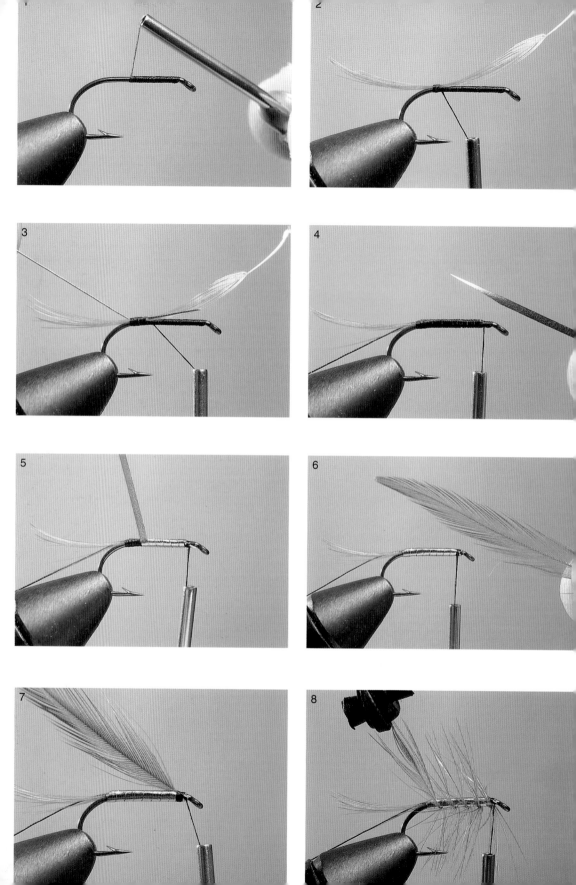

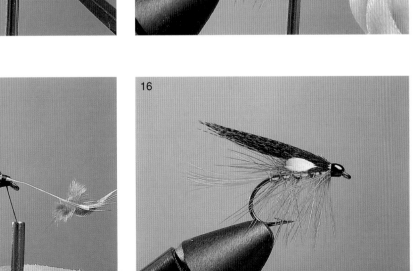

INTRODUCTION

Why have I gone to the trouble of writing another book on fly patterns when my last one, *International Guide to Trout Flies*, giving 400 dressings, was published only in 1987? The answer is simple: so much has happened in fly-tying and fly-fishing in the intervening years that a follow-up was essential.

Everything connected with fly-fishing for trout is improving all the time. Fly-tying, that infectious branch of the sport that keeps anglers going through the close season, has advanced so much that about 50 per cent of all fly-fishers now tie at least some of their flies. Such is the interest that a national monthly magazine has been launched.

Fly-tying tools and fly-hooks are all much improved on those of a few years ago, and new materials abound. Our tackle is also far better: lighter rods; better rings and reel fittings; fly-lines that help us to cast further; smarter clothing...

The famous feather for eyes in some artificial flies called jungle cock is, of course, illegal in many countries. One company in England has actually been breeding these birds domestically to get round the ban. Superb substitutes are available for feathers whose use is banned or restricted in certain countries.

A great advance, first in Britain and now on the Continent, has been in purpose-built small fisheries. Even the Scots now love the rainbow trout, realizing that it can be the backbone of sport in small fisheries close to urban centres. Many fly-fishers now favour such fisheries, and the owners of leading waters have dramatically increased the size and quality of fish stocked. Fisheries such as Dever Spring, in Hampshire, regularly produce rainbows and even browns of more than 20lb. Such fisheries, and fish, have led to new fly patterns being developed, many of them weighted, and some have become well-known as catchers of specimen trout.

Another branch of the sport which has continued to grow is competitive fly-fishing. As well as our longstanding four-country Internationals and smaller domestic events, we now have the European Grand Slam, fished in France, Belgium and England, and Small Fisheries' National Championship,

the Ladies' Internationals, and National Rivers Championship and many more. Such is the interest that it is now difficult to fish one's way through the knock-out rounds into one of the four home International teams.

The World Fly Fishing Championships are held in all the countries who have good game fishing locations. So far England, Wales, Italy, Tasmania, Finland, Poland, Spain, New Zealand, Belgium and in 1993 the memorable Canada. The venue for 1994 is Norway with at last the United States in 1995.

Competitive fly-fishing has naturally brought developments in tackle, but most of all in fly patterns. I cover many of these in this book because they are patterns used to good effect by some of our top fly-fishers. These men and women, and their flies, catch trout often in difficult conditions, and their inventive minds are doing great service to our sport.

I have been luckier than most trout fishermen in that my selection over the years for England's World, Commonwealth and European teams has taken me to fish in many different countries. New Zealand certainly lived up to Zane Grey's description of 'Fishermen's Eldorado' in both its river and lake fishing. Tasmania's central plateau remains a wilderness untouched except for the introduction of brown and rainbow trout more than 100 years ago. Their new environment, similar to New Zealand's, has seen them survive and breed in the wild perhaps better than in their native lands.

The area around Kamloops in Western Canada was a place I enjoyed visiting so much. There is magnificent sport with migratory fish in the famous Thompson and Fraser rivers and their tributaries. However, I concentrated mostly on the lake fishing, with White lake my favourite. Others included Roche, Horseshoe, Peter Hope and Knouff lakes. These produced over 500 trout to our small party in two weeks all on a catch-and-release basis. Only a few trophy fish were kept, the best a rainbow of 9lb 8oz, and an eastern brook trout I had over 4lb.

My fishing mate Charles Jardine came on the Canadian trip but he goes to America for his main fishing holiday. He keeps nagging me to go with him to Montana where he raves about the sport there.

Most people think of Spain in terms of sun-drenched holiday resorts on the costas. I think of it in terms of lovely fly-fishing rivers: the Narcia and Sella in the north with their sea-trout and salmon, and the Tormes, close to the university city of Salamanca, with its trout and non-migratory salmon known as huchen.

Finland was very different because we never knew what would take the fly next—brown trout, grayling, whitefish, perch, pike, ide or the prized migratory brown trout known as Russian browns. It was great fishing, but the midges were a nightmare. Things really are bad when you are bitten through heavy moleskin trousers.

France and Belgium are beginning to see small stillwater fisheries here and there, stocked mostly with rainbow trout. I foresee fly-fishers being more ready to travel in both directions once the Channel Tunnel is open.

But those who do not travel too far from home for their fishing can be assured that our own game-fishing, in England and Scotland, Wales and Ireland, takes some beating. I cannot think of anywhere other than an Irish lough or a Scottish loch where you can drift and take salmon or sea-trout off the top; and with salmon in rivers in all four home countries, the fly-fisher who has mastered the still-waters does not have to go too far for a new challenge—a salmon on fly.

Many of the flies featured in this book—dry flies, nymphs, lures—are patterns I have collected on my travels. Others are from my guest contributors, among them some top professional fly-dressers; and some are tied by their originators and have not been seen before. Some of the latter may not be the neatest tyings, but they all catch fish.

Together these flies will appeal to the adventurous fly-fisher/fly-tyer. They include flies for reservoirs and lakes and gravel-pits, for loughs and lochs, and for small fisheries and rivers; flies for trout and sea-trout, grayling and salmon. They include something for everyone, wherever the water, because, as I have found, trout behave and feed the same the world over.

Bob Church
1993

Professional Fly Tying Guests

GLYNN HOPPER'S SELECTION

Glynn Hopper is a professional fly-tyer from Kent who can tie as many as 300 flies in a day! Perfection is his motto, so he is never short of customers. He fishes regularly at Bewl Bridge, and it is here that he has developed many fine new patterns or sound variations of trusted favourites. He now owns a tackle-shop in Lamberhurst, on Bewl's doorstep. Here he describes some of his patterns.

1 Black Bumble

Hook: Kamasan B160, sizes 10–12–14.
Tying silk: Black.
Tag: Pearl Lurex over black thread and wet varnish.
Tail: Golden pheasant topping crest.
Body: Two strands of peacock herl.
Rib: Fine pearl Lurex.
Body hackle: Single natural or black-dyed cock hackle.
Shoulder hackle: Partridge dyed blue.
Head: Clear varnish.

This is just one of a number of new Bumble-type flies I have found useful as an early-season top dropper. I have found no advantage in using jay for the shoulder hackle; a partridge grey neck hackle dyed blue gives good movement and does the job well. I remember an enjoyable early-season session at Bewl Water. The first 'buzzers' of the season were appearing and I had three fish in five casts on the drifting, all to this fly on the dropper. I then swapped it with the Black Pennell I had on the middle and completed my limit on the same fly.

2 Hopper's Copper

Hook: Kamasan B175 short-shank, sizes 10–12–14–16.
Tying silk: Brown.
Tail: Golden pheasant tippet dyed fluorescent orange.
Body: Copper Lurex.
Rib: Copper wire.
Wing-case: Cock pheasant tail fibres dyed orange.
Thorax: Peacock herl.
Head: Clear varnish.

The combination of copper and peacock herl is a good one in this general-purpose fly. In the Benson's Regional at Bewl, six of the nine fish I had came on this pattern fished on the middle dropper. My boat partner was Bewl regular Mick Dwyer, a superb angler and good company. I have had reports of the Copper Nymph taking fish on many of the smaller stillwaters in Kent when fished on a long leader and floating line.

3 Dragonfly Nymph

Hook: Kamasan B830 medium-shank, sizes 8–10–12.
Tying silk: Black.
Tail: Two goose biots dyed olive and tied in a V.
Body: Olive seal's fur or substitute over two-thirds of the hook-length (*see* thorax).
Rib: Size 15 oval silver tinsel.
Thorax: Peacock herl over remaining one-third of the hook-length.
Hackle: Partridge grey neck dyed green-olive in the centre of the thorax.
Head: Clear varnish.

I first dressed this pattern a few years ago and it has taken a large number of fish since then. It is another fly for the long leader and floating line. It can be leaded and fished slowly with an occasional long pull alongside reed-beds. I can recall some enjoyable days at Barry Evans' fishery at Tenterden and at Darwell Reservoir in East Sussex.

---

4 Blue-dun Buzzer

Hook: Kamasan B175 or 170, sizes 10–12–14–16.
Tying silk: Black.
Head and tail: Fluorescent-white wool, Shipsman's style.
Body: Seal's fur or substitute dyed black.
Rib: Pearl Lurex and/or red wire.
Body hackle: Natural or dyed blue-dun cock.
Head: Clear varnish.

This pattern fishes well as top or middle dropper, either well stripped or left as a static dry. It is an early-season pattern when trout are up in the water, and it also fishes well as a single dry fly cast in front of rising fish. A slow figure-of-eight retrieve through a light ripple can also bring fish up to this fly.

---

5 Hopper's Fry

Hook: Long-shank, sizes 8–10–12; short-shank, size 10.
Tying silk: Black.
Underbody: Two-thirds white floss; one-third Glo-Brite 3 or 4.
Body: Pearl Mylar overall.
Rib: Silver wire.
Hackle: Cock dyed red.
Wing: A small plume of white marabou with mallard or teal over.
Head: Clear varnish.

Inspiration for this pattern came from Ken Sinfoil's fry imitation. Plenty of movement in the wing and the reflective body make this a good pattern to use when trout are fry-bashing. A floating fry at point with this on the dropper has been a productive team when fished from the bank in a good wave and left to drift. I have also had three as a team (rules size) and stripped them across moving fish, resulting in some spectacular sport. It is not a fly for light leaders, as the fish take as though they really want it!

6   Black Silverhorn (wet)

Hook: Kamasan B175, sizes 12–14–16.
Tying silk: Red.
Body: Ostrich herl dyed black; alternative, peacock herl.
Rib: Fine silver wire.
Wings: Two slips of wide pearl Lurex tied along and over body.
Hackle: Natural or dyed-black hen. (Alternative, starling with peacock herl body).
Head: Clear varnish.

I have seen large numbers of silverhorns coming off the water at Bewl from June onwards, their most noticeable feature being their steel-blue wings, which look like strips of pearl tinsel—an obvious starting point for an artificial copy. The fly works best on the top or middle dropper and cast to moving fish. Pulling with short jerks seems to produce the most violent takes. Two grizzle hackle-stalks can be tied in and swept back over the body as an addition to the dressing.

7   Black Heavy Point

Hook: Kamasan B200 nymph, size 12.
Tying silk: Black.
Shellback: Lureflash Shellback.
Body: Seal's fur or substitute dyed black.
Hackle: Natural brown hen.
Head: Clear varnish.

This pattern should be tied short, using only half the hook.

8   Orange Heavy Point

Hook: Kamasan B200 nymph, size 12.
Tying silk: Black or brown.
Body: Natural hare fur tied short and using only half the hook.
Rib: Thick copper wire.
Collar: Seal's fur or substitute dyed fluorescent orange.
Head: Clear varnish.

Devised as a sacrificial fly for loch-style fishing under International rules, and, as the name suggests, fished on the point of a three-fly team, this fly helps to turn over long leaders. The Black fishes well when pulled, and the Orange is best fished with a slow figure-of-eight retrieve, used on any line from floater to Hi-Density sinker.

DAVY WOTTON'S UNIQUE COLLECTION

I have known Davy Wotton for many years and I have long been aware that he is the 'compleat' originator and perfectionist. He is not only a top professional fly-tyer with customers world-wide, but also an International fly-fisher, having represented Wales. My picture of Davy is at the Game Fair, where he demonstrates fly-fishing. He always commands a large audience of fly-tyers hoping to pick up tips and to add to their own skills.

In 1992 Davy introduced the fly-tying world to SLF (synthetic living fibre), which is now available in forty colours in all good tackle shops. The flies in this collection may be a little more intricate than others, but they form a challenge which just has to be met and which is made easier by Davy's precise instructions.

There are two hatching and one adult caddis patterns in Davy's set. His philosophy of how the fish sees the artificial is of major importance when creating new patterns. Trying to create the ultimate fly will always be in the mind of the fly dresser, and Davy is as close as you can get with these beauties.

---

1   Dave's Fry and 2   Roach Fry

Hook: CSII JS streamer, size 2.
Tying silk: White.
Tail and inner body: Cut a four-inch length of narrow-diameter silver or pearly Mylar tube and remove the inner core. Select a pair of grey cock hackles, place them evenly together and strip off unwanted fibres to leave long stalks. Fix the tail to the Mylar by pushing the stalks into the tube and adding a drop of Superglue at the joint. Now stiffen the Mylar tube by inserting some thick nylon line smeared with Devcon Five-minute epoxy glue. Tie in this tail and body half-way down the hook-shank and trim the tail to a V-shape.
Wing: Cut a quarter-inch-thick piece of white SLF and tie it in so that the end just reaches the tail. Turn the lure over in the vice and make a belly section the same as on top. Repeat above and below a second time. Now put a lesser amount down each side. Take the half-finished fly from the vice and trim it to a fish-shape with sharp scissors. Return

the lure to the vice to add some colour. Start with some strands of light-blue or purple and then add red on the flanks to represent the little fish's fins. Finish off with a little more white and then make a neat head, tie-off and varnish.
Eyes: Crystal eyes make the lure look really special. They are clear with a dark central iris. Remove the eyes from the fine wire stem to which they are attached and glue them evenly to the head with Devcon.

The Roach Fry is a variant of Dave's Fry, using SLF in white, green, yellow and blue. Olive and brown can also be tried. Once the principle of tying the lure is mastered, you will be able to create many more variants.

Both Dave's Fry and Roach Fry imitate small fish so well they should be used when trout are known to be feeding on fry.

3   Orange Prawn and 4   Purple Prawn

Hook: Q2 Wilson lightweight singles and doubles or the Bartleet single, which is the one used in the dressing illustrated.
Tying silk: To match the fly's overall colour. I like Danville's Flymaster 6/0 or Uni-thread.
Rib: Silver or gold oval, size 14, or 6lb monofil.
Eyes: 50lb nylon and small black glass beads obtained from a dressmaker's.
Feelers: Stripped hackle stalks and goat or bucktail fibres.
Body: SLF dubbing.
Legs: SLF hank fibres.
Back: A strip of thick polythene.

The dressings are identical except for the colour change.

Prawns and shrimps are probably the deadliest bait for tempting a well-rested salmon on rivers where bait is allowed. But better-class salmon rivers almost always have a fly-only rule, and these incredibly realistic artificial prawns allow you to imitate the bait without breaking the rules. Fish them on a floating or sink-tip line in a slow, steady current and a sinker in faster-flowing streams.

Heat the ends of two inch-long lengths of 50lb nylon with a match and flatten them as they melt. Slip a glass bead on each and secure them with a dab of Superglue or Devcon. Fix the hook-point upwards in the vice and take the thread from the eye down the shank to just opposite the hook-point. Tie in a small bunch of bucktail or goat-hair, making sure it is evenly spread. Its length should be about half the hook's length. Carry on with the thread towards the bend and then go back in close turns to the eye, binding down the hair as you go.

Turn the hook the right way up in the vice and take the thread back down to just above the hook-point. Now tie in a bunch of SLF so that it faces back over the tied-in hair. Strip all the fibres off a pair of hackle feathers to leave clean stems. Secure these so that they point slightly upwards and outwards. Then bind the stalks down so that they lie along the sides of the shank.

With the eyes already fixed on to the nylon shanks, life is made easier if you flatten the nylon with a pair of pliers before you attempt to tie it in. Bind each piece of nylon alongside the hook and take the silk back to the head.

The size of the polythene shellback depends on the size of the fly being tied. A quarter-inch is about right for most sizes and it should be tied in just above the hook-point and folded down equally on either side of the hook. About ten turns of thread are needed to make it really secure.

Take the thread to mid-way down the shank, catch in a ten-inch length of 6lb nylon under the shank and bring the shortest end back towards the hook-bend. Now firmly bind down both lengths. The tying will be under some tension later on, so now is the time to make it really secure.

The next two stages demand a dubbing twister. The best I have seen is the Darrell Martin whirl, which is a 'must' for all manner of dubbing techniques. Form the dubbing loop with the silk a quarter-inch from the eye. Take the silk down to halfway down the shank, place the dubbing into the loop, and spin the SLF or seal's fur into a rope. That done, wind the rope in close, touching turns towards the bend. On a large hook, you may have to do this two or three times to complete the body, looking for a neat, chenille-like effect. The thread should now be just above the hook-point position.

For the legs, cut off a section from the SLF hank about as thick as a ball-point pen. Flatten it on the bench and grip the inch-wide strip of SLF with a Bulldog clip. Form a dubbing loop, insert the SLF, and then take the thread to the hook-eye. Spin the loop to flare the SLF like a hackle, take it down to the tying thread at the eye, and secure the loop. Carefully draw the fibres down so that they fall below the shank or, if you find this difficult, trim off the upward fibres instead.

Bring the polythene strip back over the body, secure it tightly at the eye, rib it with nylon and trim off the surplus. Now cut the tail section to length and trim the SLF legs. If you wish, you can coat the back with Devcon epoxy glue, which adds weight and translucency, especially if the fly is light green or white.

These techniques can also be used to tie smaller shrimp-style flies.

5 Mr Nasty (Alder Larva)

Hook: Long-shank, sizes 8–10, weighted with lead-wire.
Tying silk: Brown.
Tail: White marabou.
Gills: Two strands of white ostrich herl stripped down one side.
Body: Fine light-brown chenille. Finish by bringing the ostrich herl strips evenly down each flank.
Rib: Brown tying silk.
Eyes: Crystal eyes tied in figure-of-eight style with a short piece of yellow chenille.
Hackle: Dyed-yellow rabbit fur at cheeks and belly.
Thorax: Mole fur.
Head: Clear varnish.

It is said that even hungry trout cannot be tempted to eat the sedge-like adult alder fly. However, the larvae of this fly are slow-moving, inch-long meaty morsels, and the trout do eat these. An imitation such as this will catch a lot of fish off the bank early in the season when the larvae are active. Because it is weighted, it should be fished on a floating or intermediate line and long leader. Try to bounce this nymph slowly along the bottom on the retrieve.

6 Hatching Caddis No. 1 and 7 Hatching Caddis No. 2

Hook: Sizes 8–10–12–14–16–18.
Tying silk: Brown.
Body: Rusty-orange seal's fur or substitute.
Rib: Fine oval gold thread.
Wing: Blacktail deer body hair.
Shellback: Brown goose shoulder feather.
Hackle: Brown partridge or partridge dyed washed-out orange.
Head: Clear varnish.

This fly sits nicely as a dry when fished singly. If the wing is tied correctly, the fly creates a V-wake during the retrieve, giving the best of both worlds. Fish it on a floating line only.

Hook: Sizes 8–10–12–14–16–18.
Tying silk: Light brown.
Body: Rusty-orange seal's fur or substitute.
Rib: Fine gold oval thread.
Shellback: Brown goose shoulder feather.
Wing: Soft fur from hare's mask or rabbit body.
Hackle: Brown partridge or partridge dyed washed-out orange.
Head: Clear varnish.

This imitation of the hatching caddis pupa should be fished in the surface film when trout are up and taking naturals or a little deeper on an intermediate line if a hatch is anticipated in, say, early evening.

8 Adult Caddis No. 3

Hook: Sizes 8–10–12–14–16–18.
Tying silk: Brown.
Body: Rusty-orange seal's fur or substitute.
Rib: Fine oval gold thread.
Wing: Fine deerhair from inside the leg.
Thorax: Same as body, with deerhair pulled over to form shellback.
Hackle: Grey partridge dyed washed-out orange.
Head: Clear varnish.

Deerhair, correctly applied, gives enough bulk and buoyancy to keep any artificial sitting on the surface without the use of a wound-on hackle. In a big wave it is as well to add a smear of Gink to the dressing, just to make sure. This is a great evening fly which works on most stillwaters. Fish it on a floating line from early July to the end of September.

OLIVER EDWARDS' SELECTION

I have to listen to a lot of anglers' views during my fishing travels. Sometimes I have to bite my tongue as people talk nonsense, but every so often I meet someone who genuinely impresses me because his fly-tying skills and knowledge of entomology are in a league above the rest. Oliver Edwards, it could be said, is top of that league as far as river and stream fishing are concerned. Oliver, a Yorkshireman, fishes regularly on the Wharfe and the lovely Ure, and has won most of the major fly-tying competitions on offer in the angling magazines.

Oliver's book, *Imitative Fly Tying* (Merlin Unwin), will soon be on sale. I shall be one of the first to buy a copy, because I know I shall learn something new.

---

1 The Hydropsyche Larva

Hook: Partridge K4A, sizes 8–10–12–14.
Tying silk: Sue Burgess Multistrand or kevlar equivalent.
Ballast: A strip of wine-bottle lead-foil wrapped over the full body length.
Abdomen and thorax: Dingy-yellow or greyish-yellow Antron or Mohlon yarn.
Back: Brown speckled turkey; quill section.
Gills: Ostrich herl dyed grey-brown or greyish-yellow; down both sides.
Ribs: (1) 4lb breaking strain mono; (2) fine gold wire.
Legs: Three distinct clumps of partridge dyed very dark brown.

Anal tuft: Partridge filoplume or blood feather trimmed to shape.
Thorax cover: Tint first two segments with black Pantone pen.
Head: Tying thread tinted yellow with Pantone pen and clear-varnished.

The Hydropsyche caddis is an important food source for trout and grayling in fast, tumbling, free-stone streams and rivers. The larvae are particularly important during late autumn and winter, when little else is available. I tie this pattern in three sizes, 14, 12 and 10, and occasionally as large as size 8. Grayling are particularly fond of a good, big caddis larva.

---

2 The Rhyacophila Larva

Hook: Partridge K4A, sizes 10–12.
Tying silk: Sue Burgess Multistrand or kevlar equipment.
Ballast: A strip of wine-bottle foil wrapped for the full body length.
Abdomen and thorax: Bright green Antron or Mohlon yarn.
Rib: 4lb breaking-strain clear mono.
Legs: Three distinct clumps of partridge hackle dyed yellow.
Back: Tint olive with Pantone pen.
Head: Tying thread tinted yellow with Pantone pen and clear-varnished.

This pattern is now ten years old. I introduced it to the fly-fishing public through *Salmon, Trout & Sea-trout* magazine, and a number of readers took to it. One even wrote to say he had had a good day on the Wharfe with it. For those who didn't bother, let me say that this pattern is 'dynamite' for back-end trout and grayling. It is a consistent fish-puller from September to the end of the grayling season. Ideally, it should be fished close to the bottom (as should all caddis larva patterns), and my results have trebled since I started using the Roman Moser bottom-bouncing leaders.

3   Grannom

Hook: Partridge EIA dry-fly, sizes 14–16.
Tying silk: Danville's Spider Web.
Body: Fine synthetic dubbing, i.e. Ligas or Fly-Rite, black or dark brown, with a tip of mid-green as the egg-sac (optional).
Rib: Very fine gold wire.
Hackle: Genetic-quality grizzle, palmered.
Wing: Screen-printed on semi-soft plastic, cut to shape, folded, and tied in.
Antennae: Two fine tips of moose body hair or any strong, fine tapering guard-hair (optional).
Head: Clear varnish.

This super-close copy of the adult is due to the incredibly lifelike wing, and here we should ask ourselves whether the use of printed wings is really fly-tying? A few of these printed semi-soft plastic wings are on the market, but none is quite as lifelike as this Finnish product. With these superb wings, even a beginner can make a beautiful adult caddis.

Our stretch of the Wharfe has had a tremendous grannom hatch for the past few years, and this pattern was taken with total confidence the very first time it was tried. The fish was a belting grayling of 1¾lb, the angler who presented the fly being my regular partner, Bernard Benson.

4   Small Stonefly Nymph (Small Yellow Sally)

Hook: Partridge HIA nymph, sizes 16–18.
Tying silk: Danville's Spider Web, 16/0.
Ballast: A thin strip of wine-bottle lead-foil over the full body length, doubled at the thorax. Cover with thread and tint to the desired shade of yellow.
Tail: Tips of fine animal guard-hair dyed yellow or yellow-olive.
Abdomen: A thin strip of Flexibody dyed greeny-yellow.
Rib: Fine gold wire butting each turn of Flexibody.
Legs: Grey partridge dyed greenish-yellow.
Wing-buds and pro-thorax: Slightly wider strip of same colour Flexibody.

Antennae: Tips of fine animal guard-hair dyed yellow or yellow-olive.
Head: Clear varnish.

This pattern can be used generally as a small stonefly imitation or, specifically to fish when the small yellow sally (*Chloroperlatorrentium*) is emerging. The small yellow sally seems to be much the commoner of the two yellow stoneflies found in this country. Like most small nymph patterns, this one should be fished directly upstream or quartering upstream and allowed to drift back with the current, i.e. dead drift. Since most small stoneflies are similar in appearance, this pattern can be readily adapted.

5   Polywing Paradun

Hook: Partridge EIA dry-fly, sizes 14–16–18–20.
Tying silk: Danville's Spider Web.
Tail: Two or three micro-fibbets to match colour of natural's tails, i.e. olive, grey, white, dun.
Abdomen: Fine synthetic dubbing such as Ligas or Fly-Rite, the colour to match the natural's abdomen.
Thorax: Fine synthetic dubbing such as Ligas or Fly-Rite, the colour to match the natural's abdomen.
Hackle: Two or three turns of genetic-quality cock around base of wing-tuft, the colour to match the general coloration of the natural, i.e. grey, cream, blue-dun, olive.

Wing: A tuft of white or grey poly-yarn set vertically and trimmed to about the length of the natural dun's wing.
Head: Clear varnish.

This has to be one of the flies of the nineties. Parachute-style flies are becoming increasingly popular and the use of polypropylene poly-yarn for the wing, makes winding on the hackle easy and a gallows tool is unnecessary. Only the hackle on this fly is a natural product, the rest being man-made. Because the man-made fibres are virtually non-water-absorbing, this fly is a very good floater, so don't spoil its delicacy by over-hackling.

6 Sculpinhairy

Hook: Partridge bucktail/streamer GRS 4A long-shank, sizes 4–6–8–10.
Tying silk: Cream or grey kevlar type.
Ballast: 3mm strip of wine-bottle lead-foil wound in several layers on body section only and then Superglued and dorso-ventrally flattened.
Body: Dirty-grey fine synthetic dubbing.
Rib: Fine gold oval or twist.
Back and tail: Natural rabbit zonker strip, 3–4mm wide and pointed at the tail end. The zonker strip overhangs the bend by about 20mm (¾in) and is matuka-ribbed five or six times.
Pectoral fins: Speckled dark partridge smeared with flexible cement.

Head: Dark deerhair on dorsal side and light deerhair on ventral side, stacked not spun. Leave some untrimmed hairs on top and clear-varnish the tying-off.

In spring 1992 I was host to the famous American fly-tyer and fisher Dave Whitlock for a few days on the Wharfe. The river was up and slightly coloured. Dave caught a few trout and grayling on nymphs, and then, without giving it a second thought, he put on a heavy leader of 6lb breaking-strain nylon and tied on one of his Sculpin patterns, casting to the far side of the river and pausing to allow the weighted lure to sink. He hooked a huge brown of over 3lb.

7 Freshwater Shrimp

Hook: Partridge K4A, sizes 12–14.
Tying silk: Danville's Spider Web 16/0.
Ballast: A thin strip of wine-bottle lead-foil wrapped over the entire body; can be double-wrapped for heavy or deeper water.
Tail: Eight or ten fibres of grey-brown partridge hackle from the neck area.
Body: A good padding of fine synthetic dubbing, i.e. Ligas mixed with a slightly coarser Davy Wotton SLF dubbing (70 per cent fine, 30 per cent coarser). The colour is a blend of Ligas No. 14, light beige, No. 19, sand, and No. 21, pale olive, and Davy Wotton SLF No. 39, beige, with the overall colour a pale beige/olive.

Rib: 3lb breaking-strain clear or very pale-coloured mono.
Legs: Grey-brown partridge hackle-tips.
Shellback: Boat-shaped slip of clear Flexibody.
Antennae: Four or five fibres of grey-brown partridge hackle from the neck area.
Head: Clear varnish. Give the completed Shrimp a lateral squeezing with pliers before removing it from the vice.

This pattern has evolved over many years. The ability to produce short, tapering legs had always eluded me, but using the Darrel Martin dubbing whirl, the process has become quite easy.

8 Goldbody Pupa

Hook: Partridge K4A, sizes 10–12.
Tying silk: Danville's Spider Web 16/0 or standard 6/0.
Abdomen: Gold-plated beads, metallic or plastic depending on how heavy you wish the fly to be, and tapering in size. Dub liberally between each bead with a good high-glint, light-reflective dubbing such as the new Davy Wotton SLF, marketed by Partridge. Use a colour to suit the abdomen colour of the natural.
Thorax: Same as abdomen.
Wing-buds: A good pad of any dark, synthetic dubbing on the underside and up towards the sides nearing the hook-eye.

Legs: Four or five dark, ruddy pheasant-tail fibres.
Head: Tying thread tinted brown and clear-varnished.

The Goldhead went through the fly-fishing scene like the proverbial dose of salts. Within about three years, virtually every fly-box dazzled when it was opened.
This is my concession to the use of gold beads. By loading the shank with metallic and non-metallic gold-plated beads of various diameters, a tapering abdomen of sorts can be produced (the last bead on this one should be smaller). Fairly coarse, high-glint dubbing is then liberally worked between each bead.

PETER GATHERCOLE'S SELECTION

Every fly-tyer and fly-fisherman in the UK must know of Peter Gathercole, not only for his creative fly-tying and his outstanding photographs, but as a top fly-fisher. Here he has picked four families of insect which are important to stillwater fly-fishers, and his patterns feature chironomids, olives, damsels and sedges in their nymphal and winged forms. These insects are major food items for trout during spring, summer and autumn, and Peter's dressings will suit those who like their flies to be as true to life as possible and who wish to fish on or close to the surface.

---

1 CDC Thorax Dun

Hook: Captain Hamilton dry-fly, size 14.
Tying silk: Olive pre-waxed.
Tail: Blue-dun cock hackle-fibres.
Body: Medium-olive SLF.
Wing: *Cul de canard* feather.
Hackle: Blue-dun cock, clipped flush under hook.
Head: Clear varnish.

This is an effective imitation of both the pond and lake olive duns. It uses the oily feathers from around a duck's preen gland to mimic the wing of the natural. These *cul de canard* feathers, as they are known, come in a variety of shades of grey that will mimic the colour of the natural's wings. Like most dry flies, it should be given a touch of Gink and then fished on a light, degreased leader of 3–4lb breaking strain, giving good turnover and the delicacy needed to present a small fly in a lifelike manner.

For best results, the CDC Thorax Dun should be fished during a hatch of the naturals, being either left still or cast in front of a rising fish. It is so like the natural that even swifts and swallows will swoop to pick it up, letting go only as they feel the weight of the leader.

---

2 Olive Filoplume

Hook: Captain Hamilton wet-fly, size 14.
Tying silk: Olive pre-waxed.
Tail: Olive filoplume.
Rib: Fine gold wire.
Body: Olive feather-fibre.
Hackle: Olive filoplume.
Wing-case: Dark turkey feather.
Head: Clear varnish.

This highly mobile pattern is designed to imitate the nymphal stage of both the pond and lake olives. It uses the soft, downy fibres found at the base of a cock hackle to suggest the legs and gills of the natural.

Like many small nymphs, the Olive Filoplume should be fished on a floating line and a leader of 15–20ft. The effective retrieve is a series of slow, short draws or a steady figure-of-eight, although it does pay to experiment if fish are active but takes are not forthcoming.

Like the dry Thorax Dun, this nymph should be fished either during a hatch or as the precursor to a suspected hatch, when the trout could well be feeding on nymphs as they rise to the surface.

3   Traun-wing Caddis

Hook: Captain Hamilton nymph hook, size 12.
Tying silk: Brown pre-waxed.
Body: Fiery-yellow SLF.
Underwing: Deer body hair.
Hackle: Red gamecock hackle.
Wing: Brown Traun wing.
Head: Clipped deer body hair with clear-varnish tying-off.

Good hatches of the larger species of sedge, or caddis fly, seem all too rare on stillwaters these days, which is a pity, because the trout seem to prefer these larger, paler insects to the smaller, darker and more numerous species—at least as far as the adults are concerned.

The Traun-wing Caddis uses a lifelike printed wing produced by Traun River Products, of Austria. On its own the material is a little too hard, a little too clinical, and it needs the addition of an underwing of hair to break up the outline and give it life. The combination is extremely effective.

This pattern works well on both still and running water. It may be fished static or skated in the familar emerging-caddis style, mimicking the struggles of the natural as it attempts to become airborne. Fish it singly on a floating line and a tapered leader tipped with 4ft of 4lb nylon.

4   Fur-thorax Caddis Pupa

Hook: Sedge or emerger hook, size 16.
Tying silk: Brown pre-waxed.
Rib: Gold wire.
Body: Amber irise dub.
Shellback: Clear Nymph Glass.
Wing-buds: Slips of mallard primary.
Thorax hackle: Spun and clipped brown rabbit.
Antennae: Lemon wood-duck.
Head: Clear varnish.

Imagine a warm, mid-summer evening with a gentle ripple and the trout hitting something just sub-surface. What the fish are taking is obviously moving quickly, as they are bow-waving, making great swirls in their efforts to intercept their prey. They are, as likely as not, chasing caddis pupae. The movement of these highly mobile creatures is a precursor to a proper hatch, usually occuring at dusk or just after dark. Unlike chironomid pupae, caddis pupae are equipped with a pair of flattened, hair-fringed legs, or paddles, with which they are able to propel themselves at a fair old lick.

Because the trout take the pupae on their ascent, a floating line and a long leader form the most effective combination. Failing that, especially if it is very calm, an intermediate line will take the fly down a foot or so and reduce surface disturbance on the retrieve.

5   Damselfly Wiggle Nymph

Hook: Long-shank, size 10; either a specific angled pattern or a hook bent with pliers.
Tying silk: Olive pre-waxed.
Tail: Marabou dyed olive.
Rib: Fine gold wire.
Body: Medium-olive SLF.
Hackle: Grey partridge dyed olive.
Wing-cases: Olive feather-fibre.
Head: Very small lead eyes with a clear-varnish tying-off.

The well-camouflaged nymphs of the damselfly leave their weed sanctuaries from early to mid-summer before emerging as the spectacular winged adults. To complete its transition, a nymph must leave the water and crawl up a marginal feature such as a stone or reed-stem. In the open, sandy margins of a flooded gravel-pit, this often means that the nymph must break cover completely, running the gauntlet of any predatory fish. However, it is not entirely helpless and, faced with the need for a sudden dash, is able to move at a remarkable speed, propelled by rapid, lashing movements of its abdomen and tails.

Points to consider in producing an effective imitation of the damselfly nymph are colour, slimness of profile, and mobility. The Damselfly Wiggle Nymph fulfils all three, not least mobility.

6 Electric-blue Damselfly

Hook: Captain Hamilton dry-fly, size 10.
Tying silk: Black pre-waxed.
Body: Deerhair dyed blue.
Thorax: Blue SLF.
Wings: Blue-dun cock hackles.
Hackle: Blue-dun cock.
Head: Black foam with a clear-varnish tying-off.

This is not a pattern with which you are going to set the record-books alight. However, it will fill a gap, literally and metaphorically, in your fly-box. It is a pattern which you may need to use only once in three seasons. You may never have had any use for it, but if you fish shallow stillwaters in which naturals abound, then one day you will be glad of it.

The shallow, weedy margins of lakes and ponds are festooned with thousands of common blue damselflies in mid-summer, each of them on the hunt for a mate and the next meal. The trout will concentrate as often as not on the more accessible nymphs as they wiggle towards marginal vegetation. Occasionally, though, the fish will turn their attention to the adults, leaping after them as the damselflies skim over the water surface and engulfing them in mid-air in a spectacular display of fishy gymnastics.

The Electric-blue Damselfly is tied as a dry fly, so it should be fished on a floating line.

7 True-to-life Midge Pupa

Hook: Size 16 emerger.
Tying silk: Brown pre-waxed.
Breathing filaments: White marabou.
Rib: Silver wire.
Body: Black rabbit fur, ribbed with feather-fibre dyed red.
Back: Pearl Lurex.
Thorax: Grey rabbit fur.
Wing-buds: Brown goose biots, clipped to shape.
Thorax cover: Grey duck.
Head: Clear varnish.

This pattern has worked well for me on many occasions when the trout have been feeding on ascending pupae. As chironomid pupae mature, so gas is trapped between the body of the adult within and the outer skin of the pupa. This gives a silvery, sparkling appearance to the natural, a phenomenon which lends itself beautifully to imitation by a strip of pearl Lurex. Originally I used polythene to mimic this sparkle, but pearl Lurex beats it hands down.

The True-to-life Midge Pupa may be fished singly or as one of a team. A leader up to 20ft long is needed, and it must be degreased so that the fly fishes just below the surface. The pattern comes into its own in calm conditions when the trout are making sub-surface bulges as they mop up ascending naturals. Cast in front of rising fish.

8 Carpet Emerger

Hook: Captain Hamilton dry-fly, size 14.
Tying silk: Orange pre-waxed.
Rib: Pearl Lurex.
Body: Fiery-orange SLF.
Shuck: Grey polypropylene carpet fibre.
Wing: Grey polypropylene carpet fibre.
Hackle: Red gamecock.
Head: Clear varnish.

Emerger-style patterns, which sit in rather than on the surface film, have taken the stillwater trout fishing scene by storm. Where once dry-fly fishing on lakes and reservoirs was left only to the occasional crank, today it is a widely used technique.

Though they do vary considerably in size, many emergers are direct imitations of the chironomid midge, an insect at the top of the stillwater trout's menu. Over the course of a season this insect, in its various sizes and colours, must be taken literally in many millions, and anglers who neglect this otherwise insignificant looking creature do so at their peril.

Like other patterns of its ilk, the Carpet Emerger is lightly hackled, relying on a body well doused in floatant to prevent it sinking. It should be fished on a leader of at least 15ft of 4–5lb breaking strain nylon. It may be cast at rising fish or left stationary to intercept trout cruising upwind.

JEANETTE TAYLOR'S SELECTION

Jeanette Taylor is a professional fly-dresser who specializes in flies which are largely unavailable commercially, and she is asked to copy many ingenious one-off patterns which are of great interest to her as a top lady fly-fisher.

Jeanette was the first captain of the England Ladies' International Fly-fishing team. This was at a match fished against Wales at Rutland Water, and she weighed in the heaviest catch for an England win. So she can be relied upon as a fly-fisher as well as a top fly-tyer. Her latest achievement was to fish for England in the Commonwealth Fly Fishing Championships in New Zealand.

---

1 Nightingale Fly

Hook: Kamasan B175, sizes 10–12–14.
Tying silk: Black.
Tail and body: Glo-Brite fluorescent-yellow yarn No 11 or, as a variation, lime-green No 12.
Rib: Fine silver oval tinsel.
Body hackle: Palmered badger cock.
Head hackle: Badger cock slightly longer than the body.
Head: Clear varnish.

This fly came to me from Mr Nightingale, of Southport. He catches a lot of fish on it, and I have found it a great dry fly fished on a four-metre leader with a single dropper in the centre. I fish the two dry flies static, a size 14 on the point and a 12 or 10 on the dropper (according to wave height). It is not necessary to grease the leader if the flies are well rubbed with Gink. This is an advantage, especially on reservoirs, where the Nightingale can also be used as a bob-fly on the top dropper.

A size 12 fished loch-style as a point-fly, with fast pulls, did well for Bob Church at Rutland in the Midlands final, catching five of his seven fish on a difficult day.

---

2 Genie's Peach Doll

Hook: Kamasan B175, sizes 10–12.
Tying silk: Black.
Tail and back: Peach wool.
Body: Fluorescent-orange chenille.
Head hackle: Fluorescent-orange cock hackle.
Head: Clear varnish.

I wondered how I could improve the Peach Doll. Then I had the idea of using fluorescent chenille for the body. The body is bright and I still incorporate the peach wool. I have also found a variation using fluorescent lime-green chenille with a lime-green wool tail and back to be effective. I also tie the Montana Doll, with a lime-green chenille body and a black back and tail, and one with a red chenille body with a white tail and back. All catch trout at most reservoirs, but the peach one is especially effective. They can be fished on a floater and stripped through the top, or on a fast-sinker, again with a quick retrieve.

3 Flo Jo

Hook: Kamasan B175, size 10.
Tying silk: Black.
Tail: Glo-Brite fluorescent-orange floss, No 7.
Butt: Two turns of flat silver tinsel.
Body: Fluorescent-green chenille.
Thorax: Glo-Brite fluorescent-orange floss, No 7.
Wing: Black marabou.
Head: Clear varnish.

Florence Green, from Tunbridge Wells, gave me this one when we were practising at Llyn Brenig for the Ladies' International, and I tied up a couple for the next day. What a fly! The rainbows loved it!

The following night I tied up some for the whole England team, and several of them caught on it. It was later used in the Men's International, again at Brenig, when it did well.

I have since caught fish with this fly at Rutland, Grafham and Pitsford. I have also tried variations with an orange body and wing, green tail and thorax. All have worked well for rainbows in coloured or peaty water.

4 Mighty Quinn

Hook: Kamasan B175, sizes 10–12.
Tail: Short white marabou.
Body: Fluorescent-white chenille.
Rib: Fine oval copper tinsel.
Head hackle: White cock hackle.
Head: Clear varnish.

A friend and customer, Mr Pat Quinn, from Essex, asked me to tie a pattern similar to a small tadpole— but different! Yes, a bit of the Irish there!

This is the pattern I devised, and fishing it over several week-ends on a Hi-D line and pulled very fast, he came off with limit after limit. He now swears by the fly, especially when conditions are difficult.

Olive-green and black versions have also worked for him, and it has proved a great success for me at Dever Springs and on a Belgian stillwater.

5 Genie's Nymph

Hook: Bob Church Kamasan nymph, sizes 10–12–14.
Tying silk: Black.
Body: A dubbing mix of olive and orange-rust Antron.
Rib: Oval copper tinsel.
Thorax: Built-up with same dubbing as body.
Shellback: Pearl Lurex.
Head hackle: Honey cock.
Head: Clear varnish.

This season-long olive nymph is not only imitative but also has that splash of flash at the thorax. Pearl is now accepted as a great attractor of trout. This nymph excites both feeding instincts, the natural and the aggressive. Although primarily a stillwater pattern, it can be tied with an underweighted body and used for nymphing on rivers which have good hatches of olives.

6 Nairn Sedge

Hook: Kamasan B175, sizes 8–10.
Tying silk: Black.
Butt: Two or three turns of Glo-Brite floss, No 13.
Body: Emerald-green Antron, dubbed.
Rib: Fine gold oval tinsel.
Wing: Glo-Brite green yarn, No 12.
Overwing: A pinch of deerhair clipped from head and left stubby.
Head: Clear varnish.

This fly came to me from Mr Martin Nairn, of Perth, who uses it with great success on the lochs for both wild browns and rainbows. The availability of rainbow fishing has increased in Scotland during the last decade as more fishery owners have stocked them.

The Nairn Sedge has travelled south of the Border with success, and it has proved a great summer fly on all the English reservoirs on which it has been tried. Fish it on a floating line as a top-dropper bob-fly or as a stripped point-fly.

7 Pearl Buzzer

Hook: Drennan wet-fly, sizes 10–12–14.
Tying silk: Olive.
Tail: White poly-yarn.
Underbody: Olive tying silk.
Overbody: Pearl Lurex stretched and pulled tight.
Thorax: Dark-olive Antron, dubbed.
Breathers: White poly-yarn tied bow-tie style.
Head: Clear varnish.

Pearl Lurex is again used to good effect in this chironomid pupa imitation. Chironomids form the major diet of stillwater trout, rainbows and browns, from April through to September. Although the shape and silhouette are exactly right, the coloration is not. Yet the Pearl Buzzer has often outfished all others, including the popular Black and Green Buzzers.

8 Town's Dry Nymph

Hook: Sizes 12–14, up-eyed.
Tying silk: Black.
Tail hackle: Two turns of red gamecock hackle.
Body: Pheasant tail fibres.
Thorax: Fluorescent-green wool, dubbed.
Head hackle: Two turns of red gamecock.
Head: Clear varnish.

This is a pattern favoured by Mr Town, one of my regular customers. He often asks me to tie a few for him, and the rear hackle is his idea. It is just one of the dry nymphs which are currently in favour at the big reservoirs. Gink it and fish it, either singly or well-spaced out with another one, static on a floating line or with a very slow figure-of-eight retrieve.

SID KNIGHT'S SELECTION

No book on artificial flies would be complete without a new collection from Bridgnorth's professional tyer, Sid Knight. Sid has been in the business for more than twenty-five years, and a lot of creations have come from his vice. He takes great pleasure from knowing that his flies are catching big trout for his customers, and always moans that he never gets enough time to go fishing as much as he would like. Even so, I remember seeing him catch an 8lb rainbow trout at Patshall Park a few years ago. His collection clearly shows that he really likes new synthetic materials.

---

1 Pearly Rainbow Fry

Hook: Kamasan B830 long-shank, size 10.
Tying silk: Black.
Underbody: Fifteen touching turns of lead-wire tied-in on the front section of the hook.
Body: Mother-of-pearl material.
Rib: Fine silver wire.
Back: Two strands of olive Twinkle and two strands of brown Twinkle, doubled, redoubled, tied-in at the head, bent backwards, and tied-in at the tail.
Head: Clear varnish.

This Pearly Rainbow Fry has been developed to be fished in the shallow margins of stillwaters, where lots of small fish gather in the weed-beds. Whether these are minnows, sticklebacks or coarse fish fry does not seem to matter. The trick is to wade carefully and keep well away from other anglers. Stalk your fish as if you were a heron!

---

2 Pearly Gold-ribbed Hare's Ear Nymph

Hook: Kamasan B200 long-shank, size 12.
Tying silk: Black.
Underbody: Ten touching turns of lead-wire tied-in under the thorax.
Tail: Long guard-hairs from hare body fur.
Body: Hare body fur dubbed on to waxed tying thread.
Rib: Medium oval gold tinsel.
Wing-case: Strands of mother-of-pearl with the butt ends tied-in at the head and then swept back along the sides of the thorax.
Thorax: Hare body fur.
Head: Clear varnish.

Gold-ribbed Hare's Ear patterns probably have more variations than any other fly—and I have yet to find one that is no good! They all work well, and Sid's multi-use pattern is equally at home in both rivers and stillwaters. Being leaded, it is easily controlled in fast currents, getting down to the better fish. Another use is for exploring deep, dark holes where a big fish may be lying.

3 Pearly Yellow Montana

Hook: Kamasan B830 long-shank, size 10.
Tying silk: Black.
Underbody: Ten touching turns of lead-wire tied-in under thorax.
Tail: Yellow marabou with strands of mother-of-pearl Lureflash.
Body: Mother-of-pearl material.
Rib: Thin silver wire.
Wing-case: Tied-in over the thorax-olive Raffene, and better if varnished.
Thorax: Fluorescent-yellow chenille with yellow cock hackle palmered through and ribbed with the fine wire.
Head: Clear varnish.

The Pearly Yellow Montana is a favourite of Scottish fly-fishing writer Ian Muckle. Although this 'nymph lure' has such a bright coloration, it is still fished slow and deep like a nymph. It has been a winner in Scotland's peaty waters. Ian had two rainbows on it from Markle Fishery at 20lb 2oz and 19lb 1 oz—specimens indeed!

---

4 Twinkle Black Nymph

Hook: Kamasan B830 long-shank, size 10.
Tying silk: Black.
Underbody: Ten touching turns of lead-wire tied-in under the thorax.
Tail: Long black cock hackle-fibres.
Body: Three strands of black Twinkle.
Rib: Fine silver wire.
Wing-case: Hen pheasant centre tail.
Thorax: Black Twinkle tied slightly thicker than the body.
Hackle: Black cock hackle.
Head: Clear varnish.

The Black Twinkle Nymph was popular in the 1990–91 seasons, mostly on the small fisheries. It works well all over the country, but especially at Dever Springs and Avington in Hampshire. Fish it on a floating line and long leader.

---

5 Pearly Bibio

Hook: Kamasan B175, size 12.
Body: Strands of mother-of-pearl material; centre body, fluorescent-red wool.
Rib: Fine silver wire.
Hackle: Black cock hackle, palmered.
Head: Clear varnish.

Everyone knows the Bibio as a traditional Irish pattern, but Sid's variation caused quite a stir on the loughs when it outfished the original! Sid's favourite pearl Lurex is in evidence, and he reckons the extra 'flash' helps the fly to attract when it is fished as top dropper.

6 Pearly Damsel Nymph

Hook: Kamasan B200 long-shank, size 12.
Tying silk: Black.
Underbody: Ten touching turns of lead-wire tied-in under the thorax.
Tail: Insect-green marabou with strands of mother-of-pearl material.
Body: Veniard's seal's fur substitute in a mixture of five colours: olive, green, yellow, orange and hot-orange, dubbed on to waxed silk thread.
Rib: Medium oval gold tinsel.
Wing-case: Strands of mother-of-pearl material, with the butt ends tied-in at the head and then swept back and tied-in along the thorax to act as legs.
Head: Clear varnish.

Although the Pearly Damsel looks little like the real thing, it works well as a general pattern during summer, when the damsels are about in good numbers. It is an out-and-out attractor pattern that can be fished either in short, sharp twitches or stripped back as fast as you like.

7 Green Insect

Hook: Kamasan B175, sizes 12–14.
Tying silk: Black.
Body: Metallic-green Lurex.
Rib: Copper wire.
Hackle: Long-fibred insect-green cock, palmered.
Head: Clear varnish.

This metallic-green palmered insect imitation is naturally a good pattern to try if any small green midges are hatching. I have often commented to my boat partner on the metallic-green appearance of some flies that have been hatching. Thanks Sid! This one fills the bill!

8 Pearly-backed Beetle

Hook: Kamasan B175, size 12.
Tying silk: Black.
Underbody: Ten touching turns of lead-wire.
Body: Peacock herl.
Rib: Fine silver wire.
Beetleback: Mother-of-pearl material tied-down in two parts over the whole body. The first section is tied down over the back portion before the thorax is completed.
Thorax: Peacock herl tied slightly thicker than the body portion, with the butt ends of the pearly material pulled over and tied down swept back along each side of the thorax.
Head: Clear varnish.

Another weighted nymph for river or lake, the Pearly-backed Beetle could represent any beetle or bug which trout are likely to encounter throughout a season. It is a good general pattern.

CHARLES JARDINE'S SELECTION

Charles Jardine is a gifted artist, a very good fly-fisher, and a brilliantly inventive fly-tyer—and so neat! He is known throughout fly-fishing circles as a kind man, with nothing too much trouble when it comes to raising money for charity. Many of his painstakingly created original paintings have gone under the auctioneer's hammer when he could have sold them at top prices.

Charles and I produced a book called *Stillwater Trout Tactics* (Crowood), and he has written two other fine books, *Sotheby's Guide to Fly Fishing* (Dorling Kindersley) and *Dark Pools* (Crowood). He also writes in the angling press.

---

1 G.E. Nymph

Hook: TMC921, sizes 14–16, weighted at thorax.
Tying silk: Olive micro.
Tail: Three summer duck or wood-duck fibres dyed olive.
Body: Olive goose cosset or dyed pheasant tail.
Rib: Extra fine silver wire.
Thorax: Squirrel fur dyed olive and dubbed on.
Throat hackle: Summer duck or wood-duck dyed olive.
Shellback: Summer duck dyed black.
Head: Clear varnish.

This is a most delicate nymph imitation which Charles calls his general agile-darter nymph representation. Fish it in and around weed-beds with the 'induced' style of retrieve. It is a good nymph pattern to begin with if you are fishing a small river and no hatch is on. It should be used on as light an outfit as possible, with the emphasis on delicate presentation.

---

2 E.T. Buzzer (Hare's Ear)

Hook: Partridge Living Nymph GRS7; sizes 16–18–20.
Tying silk: Olive micro.
Body: Well-blended hare's mask fur in a variety of shades.
Rib: Fine pearl Mylar ribbed over shellback.
Shellback: Thin foam (as found around fruit to prevent it bruising).
Thorax: Hare's mask three times thicker than abdomen.
Thorax cover: White Polycelon; black for upwinged patterns.
Head: Clear varnish.

It is rare to find anyone using such a tiny nymph on reservoirs. This is a sparse, more natural-looking Suspended Pupa which should be fished delicately on the finest leader and retrieved as slowly as possible. Sometimes it is best left static, especially if a breeze drifts it along.

3 Lively Mayfly

Hook: Grub size 10.
Tying silk: Yellow or light-olive micro.
Tail: Pheasant tail fibres.
Body: Detached body of white deerhair fibres with a thorax of cream seal's fur substitute.
Rib: Tying silk.
Wing: Wood-duck dyed yellow.
Hackle: Badger or grizzle.
Head: Clear varnish.

This is a great newly hatched mayfly pattern for river, lake or lough, and a proven winner from the Test to Lough Conn. I have the greatest faith in it when I fish it by itself and dry during a mayfly hatch, and even at mayfly time, when nothing is hatching. The white deerhair detached body makes the fly unsinkable, and it is very good in disturbed water, such as a high wave on a lough.

4 The Wretched Mess (Hare's Ear)

Hook: TMC100 Drennan Emerger or Partridge E6A (Hopper dry), sizes 12–14–16–18.
Tying silk: Primrose ultra-fine micro.
Tag: Five or six strands of orange seal's fur substitute.
Body: Well-mixed blended hare's mask, dubbed fairly sparsely.
Wing: White *cul-de-canard* flanked by two small slivers of pearl Lureflash Mobile.
Thorax: Hare's mask fur, as body.
Hackle: Ginger cree wound through thorax.
Head: Clear varnish.

Lots of new patterns have been devised following the dramatic increase in interest in dry-fly fishing on large reservoirs. This is Charles's first choice, and it works well in the modern dry-fly midge theme. Fish it with confidence throughout the day, with chances still good with a wave on.

5 Sparkle Gnat

Hook: TMC16–20 Partridge or Hopper dry, sizes 16–18.
Tail: Three strands of pearl Twinkle.
Body: One strand of peacock herl; two strands for larger hooks.
Hackle: Grizzle hackle palmered down whole body.
Head: Clear varnish.

The Sparkle Gnat can give good results during a chironomid hatch. It has good visibility, allowing a perfect strike when a take comes. It can be fished singly or two or three together, well spaced. I use three in a big wave; two in a smaller wave; and one in a flat calm. This tactic seems to keep the catch-rate up. It certainly did at the back-end of the 1992 season at Rutland Water, when Charles caught some difficult but memorable fish from the bank.

6 Annabelle

Hook: Kamasan B175, size 10.
Tying silk: Primrose.
Tail: Hot-orange or fluorescent-yellow Glo-Brite floss.
Body: Gold Lurex.
Rib: Fine gold wire.
Body hackle: Light ginger cock, palmered.
Head hackle: Grizzle cock.
Head: Clear varnish.

Used as an enticer top dropper from a boat in a perfect wind and a good wave, this pattern is best suited to the larger reservoirs, where good, fit rainbows are regularly encountered in mid-summer and autumn. Use it with a floating, sink-tip or intermediate line. Hold the 'bob' for several seconds after retrieving.

7 Duck's Dun (Pond Lake Olive)

Hook: TMC921 or E1A sizes 14–16.
Tying silk: Primrose micro.
Tail: Three, four or five fibres of grizzle hen or jungle-cock spade feather.
Body: Light-yellow-olive Hairtron or soft Antron.
Wing: Two *cul-de-canard* feathers, back to back and upright.
Hackle: Dark-blue dun wound through thorax and clipped to a V underneath.
Head: Clear varnish.

Olives are so common on our reservoirs, gravel-pits and loughs that you cannot fail to see them hatching on almost every trip from May onwards. The use of *cul-de-canard* feathers as wings in this dressing helps to make it a perfect, delicate, non-sinkable dry olive. Fish it singly on a fine leader point. If a size 14 hook is used, a well-spaced dropper can be added carrying an emerging olive nymph. This dry fly can also be used on rivers where olives are found the whole year through.

8 Sunset Spinner

Hook: Partridge L3A, 14A or E1A, sizes 14–16–18.
Tying silk: Maroon micro.
Tail: Two white nylon paintbrush bristles (Daler oil 8 or 10), widely spaced.
Body: Well-mixed rust-orange Poly 11, red-brown Poly 11 and red body floss or Antron in proportions of five: four: one; built up slightly for the thorax.
Rib: Lurex, Lureflash or Flashabou (optional).
Wings: Two good-quality blue-dun cock hackles wound together through the thorax and clipped to a V top and bottom, with the option of two strands of pearl Twinkle tied spent.
Head: Clear varnish.

The synthetic materials which Charles has used here give a lovely spent dry fly. It began as a Blue-winged Olive Spinner, but the body imitates any insect hatching during evening. It is purely an evening fly, the red echoing the red spectrum which the trout sees and selects at that time of day.

MICKY BEWICK'S SELECTION

Micky Bewick, from north London, is a fly-tyer and fly-fisher I have admired for a number of years. Some of his catches from the Queen Mother Reservoir, near Heathrow, have been first-class. In the late 1980s he began to enter a number of national and international competitions, and his results were consistently good both at home and on the Continent.

Micky is recognized as the man who developed the Booby method into a style for catching specimen trout. I think he will be an England team man before long. His set of personally tied flies are all proven winners, and he tells how to use them.

---

1 Yellow Plastazote Booby

Hook: Kamasan B175, size 8.
Tying silk: Sparton yellow micro.
Tail: Buttercup-yellow marabou.
Body: Yellow chenille.
Head: Yellow Plastazote, three-quarters-of-an-inch long by one-quarter square, tied in figure-of-eight style and trimmed round on each side with sharp scissors. Clear varnish over normal whip-finish.

I devised this pattern in 1986 after acquiring a yellow Plastazote swimming float. It was one of those patterns that went into the box and was forgotten after being tried unsuccessfully. Then one autumn day at Queen Mother Reservoir, when things had been rather quiet, on went the Yellow Booby. I cast out, waited a couple of minutes for it to sink, and then, as I began a figure-of-eight retrieve, had one gentle pull before everything went solid. I had no need to set the hook. The fish had taken so hard that it had hooked itself. It was a beautiful silver fish of 5lb 2oz and was followed by others of 4lb 10oz and 3lb 3oz.

I gave some Boobies to Chris Dawn, editor of *Trout Fisherman*, and he later caught a near 8lb brown trout at Rutland Water on an all-yellow.

---

2 Green Squirrel Nymph

Hook: Kamasan B175, sizes 10–12.
Tying silk: Olive-green.
Tail: Pheasant tail feather-fibres dyed olive-green.
Body: Fluorescent lime-green floss.
Thorax: Squirrel fur dyed olive-green.
Wing-case: Pheasant tail feather-fibres dyed olive-green.
Head: Clear varnish.

Squirrel fur is little used by fly-tyers, though some very good dyed squirrel pelts are available. Squirrel is easy to use for dubbed bodies. It pulls off the skin easily and has more guard-hairs than hare or rabbit.

I tied this nymph for Dever Springs, where it worked well. It has also worked well on concrete-bowl reservoirs such as Queen Mother and Farmoor II. Fish it early in the season on a floating line and very long leader. My best results on these reservoirs have come when the wind has been at my back. Takes on the drop are not uncommon.

3 The Jet

Hook: Kamasan B175 for heavyweight version; B170 for surface version; sizes 10–12.
Tying silk: Olive green.
Body: Squirrel dyed olive-green; red seal's fur substitute in the middle; and then olive-green squirrel again.
Rib: Fine gold wire.
Hackle: Olive-green hen.
Head: Clear varnish.

I named this fly the Jet because green and red are the colours of my local ice-hockey team, the Jets. Apart from tying flies in the close season, I also watch hockey. It is nearly as good as fishing!

This fly is a real all-rounder—very good fished on a light hook in the surface film or as a good, heavy point-fly tied on a heavyweight hook. I have also had success with it as middle dropper on a Hi-D line and fished hang-lock-style. It is also a good top dropper if all the guard hairs are combed out to make it bushy.

My fishing pal, Jim Longmore, used the Jet to good effect to win a match against the Army Angling Club at Rutland, using it on short drifts into the shallows at the top of the South Arm. Jim quickly caught eight trout. Four took second place!

4 Micro-chenille Buzzer

Hook: Kamasan B175, sizes 8–10.
Tying silk: Brown.
Body: Reddish-brown micro-chenille tied in at the bend.
Wing-buds: Jungle cock or yellow goose biot.
Thorax: Reddish-brown micro-chenille.
Head: Clear varnish.

I love playing around with new materials, and when I noticed this in a tackle-shop, I thought it interesting and I couldn't wait to get to my fly-tying bench to experiment. Micro-chenille is so fine when wound on the hook that it gives the appearance of a herl body. But unlike herl of any kind, micro-chenille is almost indestructible. When I have shown people flies tied with this new chenille, no one has guessed that they are made of a synthetic.

This reddish-brown Buzzer works well as a point fly in a team of three. A heavyweight hook puts it lower in the water. It has worked well at Rutland from boat and bank, but especially in late May in the South Arm.

5 Peach Nymph

Hook: Drennan nymph, sizes 12–14.
Tying silk: White micro.
Tail: Six pheasant tail feather-fibres.
Body: Peach wool.
Rib: Pearl Mylar.
Thorax: Peach wool.
Wing-case: Pheasant tail feather-fibres.
Head: Clear varnish.

This nymph came about by accident at the time when everyone was tying Peach Baby Dolls after Brian Leadbetter had won the World Championship when he had used that fly to good effect at Rutland and Grafham.

I pulled a strand of peach wool into three and then thought I could make a much sparser fly by using these thin pieces of wool. The trout at my local reservoir had been feeding heavily on newly hatched fry, and the Peach Nymph, with its pearly rib, is perfect on such occasions. The nymph caught me rainbows of 8lb 6oz, 8lb and 7lb 15oz—all grown-on from 1lb, not stockies.

6 Datchet Razzler

Hook: Drennan long-shank nymph, size 8.
Tying silk: White.
Tail: White marabou, one-and-a-half-times the length of the hook.
Body: White Plastazote glued to the shank with Araldite Rapid and trimmed to shape.
Head: White deerhair trimmed to shape with clear varnish over normal whip-finish.

This is a variant of the Razzler. I first tied it in the late seventies, when it proved the most effective fly I had ever used for big rainbows. Fished on a Hi-D line, it can be slowly stripped or retrieved figure-of-eight style. It is especially useful when trout are fry-feeding deep down.

The tail of my original pattern was made of cock hackle-fibres. Then, after a good afternoon at Queen Mother Reservoir, I gave the fly to Roy Palmer, of Iver Fly fishers, who could not believe how good it was. Copying the fly, Roy substituted marabou for the tail, which improved it tremendously.

7 Micro-chenille Black-and-red Spider

Hook: Kamasan B175, sizes 12–14–16.
Tying silk: Black micro.
Body: Black micro-chenille with a hot-spot of red micro-chenille in middle.
Hackle: Two or three turns of black hen.
Head: Black or clear varnish.

This is another touch-bodied fly, and it has worked well for me at Bewl Water in early summer when the trout have contained a lot of tiny black beetles.

I am sure this versatile chenille is going to gain in popularity. It is available in sixteen colours and is now in almost all tackle-shops.

8 Duck-gland Buzzer

Hook: Kamasan B400, sizes 12–14.
Tying silk: To suit colour of body.
Body: Condor substitute; black, red, brown or claret.
Rib: Fine pearl Mylar.
Head: Three duck gland feathers tied in a loop with clear varnish over normal whip-finish.

I have never been happy with my polystyrene-ball Suspender Buzzer, but this one could not be simpler to tie. It looks so natural in the water, with the almost unsinkable duck-gland feather breaking through the surface like the insect's legs and wing-case when it is ready to hatch. Nick Cook used a similar version of this fly to come fourth in the Belgian European Open. He would have won the event easily if he had landed only half the fish he hooked. This is a tying style of the future for small emerger flies.

BOB CHURCH'S FAVOURITES

Favourite flies, nymphs and lures come and go with all fly-fishers, and I am no different. These eight are patterns that did well for me in 1992. By the time this is read, they could be only memories—with just a few patterns in my fly-boxes in case I do need them.

---

1 Pinnegar's Buzzer

Hook: Sizes 10–12.
Tying silk: Black.
Tag: Fluorescent-white floss.
Body: Black floss.
Rib: A thin strip of strong, clear plastic.
Wing-cases: Orange synthetic raffia.
Thorax: Black rabbit fur dubbed on.
Breather: Fluorescent-white floss.
Head: Clear varnish.

One early-season day at Ringstead Grange I watched John Pinnegar, from Coventry, fishing Buzzer Nymphs on a slow retrieve. His success was such that he caught twenty-four trout when others caught only two or three. He gently returned all but his allowed six-fish bag.

I was naturally inquisitive to know what his particular Buzzer looked like, and he kindly gave me a couple to try. Since then I have caught many trout on this simple nymph. It seems to work at all still-waters when fished almost static, by which I mean with an inched retrieve.

---

2 Solwick

Hook: Sizes 10–12–14.
Tying silk: Black.
Tail: Ginger cock hackle-fibres.
Body: Rear half, flat gold tinsel; front half, bright red seal's fur or substitute.
Rib: Fine gold oval thread.
Body hackle: Ginger cock hackle, palmered.
Head hackle: Dark ginger cock.
Head: Clear varnish.

The Soldier Palmer and Grenadier have been first-choice palmered bob flies for many years, but for me these two reliable patterns have been bettered at Rutland and Grafham by the Solwick. The fly is half Soldier Palmer and half Wingless Wickham's, and one big-wave day at Rutland, drifting in the North Arm, it took fish after fish for me, with other flies on the cast ignored.

3 Detached-body Hawthorn

Hook: Sizes 12–14, lightweight.
Tying silk: Black.
Tail and back: Rib a thin strip of black Plastazote to be pulled back later for the shellback.
Body: Black seal's fur or substitute.
Legs: Black feather-fibre.
Hackle: Black hen.
Wing: A pair of white cock hackle-tips.
Shellback: Pull a strip of black Plastazote over the body and secure (already tied in at tail).
Head: Black varnish.

I always enjoy the second week of May, when the hawthorn flies arrive in earnest. They are about on and off for the rest of the month according to weather conditions, and on cloudy, windy days lots of them are blown on to the waters. Trout love hawthorn, and I like to match the naturals with a good dry artificial. If you catch the right day, you can have some of the best sport of the whole year.

4 The Dabbler

Hook: Sizes 8–10.
Tying silk: Black.
Tail: Cock pheasant tail feather-fibres.
Body: Claret seal's fur or substitute or Antron.
Rib: Fine gold oval thread.
Body Hackle: Claret cock hackle, palmered.
Wing: Natural bronze mallard with two slips of pearl Crystal added.
Hackle: Natural bronze mallard.
Head: Black varnish.

When I arrived at Lough Melvin, in County Donegal, to fish the spring International, the talk was of one fly: the Dabbler, an invention of an angler from the Dromore club. Several versions of the fly exist, but it is the claret one which is most favoured on the loughs. England won the match handsomely—with a little help from an Irish fly!

5 O'Keefe's Smelt

Hook: Long-shank Tinhead sizes 8–10, painted bright red. Add extra lead-wire to body shank.
Tying silk: Olive or brown.
Tail: Long fibres of rabbit body fur.
Body: Dubbed rabbit body fur.
Rib: Copper wire.
Wing: Four short strands of pearl Crystal.
Head: Clear varnish.

This lure was given to me by Mr O'Keefe, a Roturua tackle-dealer, when I was in New Zealand. My second cast with it on Lake Rerewhakaaitu resulted in a 4lb rainbow. The lure looks nothing until it is in the water, when the rabbit fur becomes mobile. It was intended to imitate a smelt in New Zealand, but it has caught fish for me at Rutland, Grafham and Pitsford, so it travels well. Use it with confidence anywhere where trout are known to feed on small fish. Mr O'Keefe's original fly was not a Tinhead, it just had fluorescent-red floss tied in at the head.

6 Corrib Spider

Hook: Size 10.
Tying silk: Black.
Body: Flat silver tinsel.
Rib: Fine silver oval thread.
Hackle: Long fibres of natural black hen.
Head: Clear varnish.

I discovered this deadly Lough Corrib pattern at duckfly time (March/April) in 1990. The duckfly is a big, black chironomid, and the wild browns rise well to it. We had difficulty in tempting takes until Paul Harris found a scruffy old pattern in his box and gave it a try. The result was lots of offers. We tied some up that night and did well the next day. When the big, black duckfly, buzzer or midge (call it what you will) is on the water, this simple pattern takes some beating, but you do need a fair breeze to get the best from it. Fish it at top dropper on a floating line.

---

7 Belgian Barbel Nymph

Hook: Size 10 with silver-plated brass ball attached and secured.
Tying silk: Black.
Tail: Cock pheasant tail feather-fibres.
Body: Rear half, cock pheasant tail feather-fibres; front half, black seal's fur or substitute; carrot-shaped.
Head: Clear varnish tying-off.

This simple nymph was given to me by a Belgian fly-fisher when I fished with him in the European Championship at Ardleigh, near Colchester. He had told me that he fished his local river with this nymph and made big catches of barbel. 'The nymph is so good that it outfishes those using bait,' he said. I have tried it with great success on small fisheries such as Dever Springs and Avington, with takes on the drop common. Now I must find time to try it for barbel on the Great Ouse!

---

8 Tiny Goldhead

Hook: Size 14.
Tying silk: Orange.
Tail: Light-olive cock hackle-fibres.
Body: Rear half, medium-olive seal's fur or substitute; front half, fluorescent-orange seal's fur or substitute.
Shellback: Bright orange feather-fibres over gold head.
Head: Clear varnish tying-off.

This is a pattern to try when the fish have seen everything else. It was a 'secret weapon' for me in 1992, when I found that while everyone fishing with larger flies at the small fisheries had slow sport, although the fish were there, this nymph fished slow and deep brought good results.

CHRIS OGBORNE'S SELECTION

I have known Chris Ogborne for twenty years, during which time he has been a fierce and respected competition opponent and a close colleague when we fished together for England in several Internationals, European Grand Slams and World Championships. We had more than our fair share of success with World Championship gold in 1987 and European Grand Slam gold in 1990.

Chris is the leading personality of the Bristol fly-fishers who fish those two lovely stillwaters, Chew Valley and Blagdon. He prides himself on devising new fly patterns, and his variations of known patterns are sometimes far better than the originals.

---

1 Shellback Shrimp

Hook: Grub hook, sizes 10–12.
Tying silk: Black.
Underbody: Build up a 'shrimp' shape with layers of lead-wire.
Body: Natural hare's ear.
Middle body: One turn of fluorescent-green wool.
Back: Fine gold wire.
Beard: A sparse false hackle of teal or wood-duck fibres.
Head: Clear varnish.

One of the most effective 'new' patterns of recent seasons, this one has 'worked' on fisheries as far apart as Dever Springs in England and Flaxy Lake in New Zealand. It is an ideal fly for 'Polaroiding' tactics on small stillwaters, but is also effective on rivers. Even the Yorkshire grayling seem to like it. It must be well leaded and is best fished as a single fly on a very long leader.

---

2 Black Pheasant Tail

Hook: Partridge nymph hook (HIA), size 12.
Tying silk: Black.
Tail: A pinch of teal fibres.
Body: Pheasant tail fibres dyed black.
Rib: Fine silver wire.
Thorax: Build up a bulky thorax of pearly tinsel.
Wing-case: Black pheasant tail fibres.
Beard: A false hackle of teal fibres.
Head: Clear varnish.

This is one of the most successful variations of the Pheasant Tail theme, and is one of the best pulling flies in my box. It can be fished on floaters or sinkers, at all depths and at all speeds of retrieve—truly a versatile fly. It is ideal when pin-fry are about, but works equally well as a general suggestive pattern when no fly-life is obvious on the water.

3   Shellback Hare's Ear

Hook: Partridge nymph hook (HIA), sizes 10–12.
Tying silk: Black.
Tail: Olive wood-duck fibres.
Body: Natural hare's ear.
Rib: Fine gold wire.
Wing-case: Spectraflash.
Thorax: Natural hare's ear.
Hackle: Olive wood-duck tied as legs, with a small pinch on either side.
Head: Clear varnish.

This new variation incorporates the superb Spectraflash to improve on an established favourite. Best used weighted, this is a fly for all waters and for all times of year. It is suggestive rather than imitative, and is particularly useful when fished deep and slow.

---

4   Pearl and Peacock

Hook: Partridge living nymph hook, sizes 14–16.
Tying silk: Black.
Tail: Two strands of natural pheasant tail fibre.
Body: A single strand of peacock herl.
Rib: Very fine pearly tinsel.
Wing-case: Pheasant tail fibres.
Thorax: Pearly tinsel.
Head: Clear varnish.

Clear proof that some of the best things in life are the simplest, this little pattern could not be easier to tie. It is ideal when the fish are really fussy in both still and running water. It is a great sub-surface nymph and will tempt even the most selective feeders.

---

5   Improved Black Hopper

Hook: Kamasan B400, sizes 10–12.
Tying silk: Black.
Body: Black seal's fur or substitute, tied slim.
Rib: Medium pearly tinsel.
Legs: Six knotted black pheasant tail fibres.
Hackle: Two turns of dark grey.
Head: Clear varnish.

This is an excellent version of the ever-popular Black Hopper, and one that has more colour and life for brighter days. The little red butt seems to pull in the fish, and the tinsel rib adds a degree of sparkle for good measure. The fly fishes best in a combination of good wave and bright sun. It is not a fly for flat calms or dull conditions.

6   Black Buzzer

Hook: Partridge Captain Hamilton wet fly or Kamasan B170, sizes 12–14–16.
Tying silk: Black.
Butt: Two turns of deep red or scarlet wool.
Body: Black Easy Dub (Veniard).
Rib: Fine gold wire.
Thorax: Two strands of peacock herl.
Wing-case: Pheasant tail fibres.
Breathers: Small tufts of fluorescent-white wool.
Head: Clear varnish.

This is one of my best patterns and it has stood the test of time better than any other. It is for all classic buzzer conditions, either a daytime rise or late in the evening. I carry it in all sizes. The new Easy Dub body material makes it a lot easier to tie than the old seal's fur version.

7   Shuck Fly

Hook: Partridge dry fly (fine wire), sizes 12–14.
Tying silk: Black.
Tail: A few wisps of cream seal's fur or substitute; long strands.
Shuck: Cut the shape of a shuck from Ethafoam and catch it in with a few turns of orange tying silk.
Head: Clear varnish.

Fish feed freely on shucks far more often than many people think, and the Shuck Fly can really score when they are cruising in the surface film and when conventional dries do not work. It is simple to tie and should be fished just as any other stillwater dry pattern. On really hard days, I use it as a single dry on a very long leader.

8   Green Tag Stick

Hook: Heavy-wire nymph hook, standard or long-shank, sizes 10–12–14.
Tying silk: Black.
Butt: Two turns of fluorescent-green wool.
Body: Three strands of peacock herl.
Rib: Gold wire or gold oval thread.
Hackle: Two turns of soft badger hen.
Head: Clear varnish.

No selection of mine would be complete without the ubiquitous Green Tag Stick, one of my very best flies. It has won competitions on virtually every lake in the land. In fact, it has worked wherever I have used it anywhere in the world. Its secret lies in the 'life' given by the soft hen hackle, used in preference to the stiff cock hackles that many people use. It must move as the fly is retrieved. It is a fly for all waters, all times of year, and all conditions.

PETER COCKWILL'S SMALL FISHERY SELECTION

Peter Cockwill has specialized in catching big fish from small fisheries, taking many double-figure rainbows of 20lb and more. He won the Wilcon Classic Competition at Dever Springs in both 1989 and 1990 in a seeded field of twenty-four International fly-fishers.

Peter's flies and nymphs are very simple, but the most effective patterns usually are. He has designed all of them to catch fish from small fisheries, mostly in the South of England. He writes regularly in the angling press and has his own tackle-shop in Surrey.

---

1 Leaded Bug

Hook: Short-shank, size 10.
Tying silk: Olive.
Tail: Pearsall's olive floss.
Body: Two inches of 0.35mm lead-wire wound in tight coils.
Thorax: Pearsall's olive floss.
Throat legs: Pearsall's olive floss.
Head: Clear varnish.

This pattern is intended to suggest a basic nymph outline and to sink quickly without carrying too much bulky lead. It is best fished by being cast to targeted trout and then pulled away to induce a take.

---

2 Hi-spot Lead

Hook: Short-shank, size 10.
Tying silk: Olive.
Tail: Olive hen hackle-fibres.
Body: Two inches of 0.63mm lead-wire wound in tight coils.
Thorax: Fluorescent lime-green chenille.
Hackle: Olive hen.
Head: Clear varnish.

The Hi-spot fishes well in deep water. Such places almost always hold a big trout or two, but they are difficult to see. But if you can see your nymph, you know what's going on—such as a fish following.

3 Teeny Nymph

Hook: Short-shank, size 10, with underbody weight of two inches of 0.35mm lead-wire.
Tying silk: Olive.
Body: Pheasant-tail fibres dyed olive and ribbed with olive tying silk (optional).
Body hackle: Dark-olive hen hackle-fibres.
Throat hackle: Dark-olive hen hackle-fibres.
Head: Clear varnish.

The famed American fly-fisher, Jim Teeny, devised this version of the Pheasant Tail. It can be used in various situations, but it imitates a dark shrimp very well.

---

4 Hare's Ear Shrimp

Hook: Short-shank, sizes 10–12, with underbody weight of two inches of 0.35mm lead-wire.
Tying silk: Olive.
Body: Dubbed hare's mask fur, kept very thick.
Rib: Oval copper thread.
Head: Clear varnish.

This shrimp uses the Hare's Ear idea, but is tied very fat. It is excellent for takes on the drop. Sometimes it catches too many unwanted stock fish, but it can also tempt a specimen.

---

5 Green-tail Damsel

Hook: Long-shank, size 10, with underbody weight of two inches of 0.35mm lead-wire.
Tying silk: Olive.
Tail: A one-inch length of fluorescent lime-green wool well picked out.
Body: A mixture of olive and brown seal's fur or substitute dubbed on.
Rib: Fluorescent lime-green floss pulled tight.
Hackle: Partridge dyed yellow.
Head: Clear varnish.

This pattern, devised from a tying by Terry Griffiths, is excellent in coloured water when little else seems to work. Fish it slow and deep.

6   *Grey Peacock Nymph*

Hook: Short-shank, size 10, with underbody weight of one inch of 0.35mm lead-wire.
Tying silk: Olive.
Tail: Grey feather-fibres.
Body: Grey feather-fibres.
Thorax: Grey feather-fibres.
Shellback: Grey feather-fibres.
Head: Clear varnish.

All the feather-fibres for this simple bland-grey nymph are taken from the underside of the peacock's tail. It looks like a chironomid and sinks quickly.

7   *Hole-in-the-Weed Fly*

Hook: Long-shank, size 10.
Tying silk: Olive or white.
Tail: White marabou feather-fibre.
Body: Two inches of 0.63mm lead-wire wound in tight coils.
Hackle: White marabou feather-fibre, a bunch on top and a bunch beneath the shank.
Head: Clear varnish.

This is known as the Hole-in-the-Weed Fly because it was first designed to be dropped through tiny clear patches in mats of floating algae, where it was jigged up and down. It solved the problem of fishing in places where no one else would dream of trying—and it worked!

8   *Marabou Lead Bug*

Hook: Short-shank, size 10.
Tying silk: Olive or white.
Tail: A few strands of very short white marabou feather-fibre.
Body: Two inches of 0.35mm lead-wire wound on in tight coils.
Wing: A short spray of white marabou feather-fibres.
Head: Clear varnish.

The Marabou Lead Bug sinks very quickly because of its sparse dressing, but it retains plenty of action. It is ideal when finer leaders are needed for spooked trout.

JEREMY HERRMANN'S SELECTION

Over six years I have watched Jeremy Herrmann, from Market Harborough, develop from being a member of the England Youth Fly Fishing team into a top-class performer. He is young and enthusiastic and won several major competitions in 1991. He is a superb long caster and an inventive fly-tyer. These are his patterns and his comments.

1 Black Leadhead

Hook: Kamasan B830, size 8, leaded with fine lead-wire or shot.
Tying silk: Black.
Tail: Various colours of marabou.
Body: Various colours of fine chenille. See text for colour combinations.
Head: Clear varnish.

This 'family' of flies probably catches more reservoir trout each season than any other. Indeed, the 'Doggie' is so deadly that some anglers cringe at the sound of its name, saying: 'Oh, I thought you caught it on a proper fly!' However, the same fly seems perfectly acceptable if it is referred to as a Leaded Tadpole. Why I don't know. My own method of fishing these lures is on a Wet-Cel 11 line with a 20ft 5lb leader and with a constantly varied retrieve. This is the most effective way of catching stockies, and it also accounts for many better resident fish.

My innovation with Leadheads is not so much in the materials as in the aspect which makes the fly so effective—the leading. The original Dog Nobblers were tied with a shot pinched on at the head. I tie mine in three ways. First, the old way is still good and gives a pronounced up-and-down motion on the retrieve. Second, I use fine lead-wire along the body, but with the bulk of the lead built up in a ball at the head.

2 Monty Nymph

Hook: Kamasan B830, size 10, leaded with fine lead-wire wrapped evenly up and down the shank.
Tying silk: Fluorescent lime-green.
Butt: Fluorescent lime-green tying silk.
Underbody: Fluorescent lime-green tying silk.
Body: Black seal's fur or substitute.
Rib: Silver wire.
Thorax: Black feather-fibre.
Head: Fluorescent lime-green tying silk with clear varnish.

Every keen stillwater fly-fisherman has his own variation of the deadly Montana Nymph. This is mine, and it has accounted for a sickening number of trout over the years. It is best tied quite heavily leaded and fished as a point-fly, either singly or in a team of three on a floating line.

Its beauty is that the more you catch on it, the more the fish seem to want it. It is tied with lime-green silk, so when the trout have shredded the seal's fur or substitute with their teeth, the fluorescence glows through and seems to improve the appearance of the fly. As with all really good flies, this one is as effective on the wiser resident fish as it is on stockies.

Rutland is where the Monty was born and bred, as a more lifelike development of the traditional Montana.

3 Fuzzy Duck

Hook: Kamasan B175, size 12.
Tying silk: Fluorescent lime-green.
Butt: Fluorescent lime-green silk.
Body: Fluorescent lime-green floss.
Rib: Silver wire.
Body hackle: Palmered red game.
Head hackle: Grey partridge.
Head: Clear varnish.

The Fuzzy Duck is a cross between a Soldier Palmer and a Partridge and Green, and it is my favourite middle-dropper for floating-line fishing. It has accounted for hundreds of trout for both myself and my friends. Its strength is that not only does it look edible, but it combines the deadly colours of fluorescent lime-green and ginger.

My favourite wet-fly team for summer fishing with a floating line includes this fly on the middle dropper, with a Soldier Palmer above and either an Orange Seal's Fur Nymph or The Usual below. This team is my standby on waters I do not know, and it is unbeatable at Draycote, where the trout are always hard on red- or green-coloured flies. With both on your cast, you can't fail!

One particularly memorable evening with the Fuzzy was at Blagdon in 1991. I arrived at the North Shore at about seven o'clock on a balmy summer evening and made a tremendous catch.

4 Blakeman's White Lure

Hook: Kamasan B800, size 8, leaded with seventy-two turns of fine lead-wire wrapped evenly up and down the body.
Tying silk: White.
Tail: White marabou.
Body: White fine Sparkle chenille.
Wing: Three plumes of marabou spaced evenly along the body, with several strands of pearl Flashabou in the one nearest the eye.
Head: Clear varnish.

This lure is an invention of a good friend and regular fishing partner, Tony Blakeman, from Coventry. He devised it a couple of seasons ago and we have both had some great catches on it. It is not only a great fry-imitator, but also an extremely effective catcher of stockies. It is frequently taken on the drop.

The secret of this lure is again in the leading. Tony insists that it works at its best with exactly seventy-two turns of lead wound evenly back and forth along the body.

Who am I to argue, having caught more than forty trout on the first Blakeman's White he gave me before it was taken by a pike? The Wet-Cell 11 with a long leader is again best. However, I have also done well on a Wet-Cel Intermediate.

This fly has given me many memorable catches.

5 Jungle-cock Claret Emerger

Hook: Kamasan B170, size 12.
Tying silk: Black.
Body: Dark-claret seal's fur or substitute.
Rib: Pearl Flashabou.
Thorax: Dark-claret seal's fur or substitute.
Cheeks: Jungle cock or substitute.
Hackle: Very dark red game; bottom half clipped.
Head: Clear varnish.

No selection of modern flies is complete without a dry fly. Dry-fly fishing has increased in popularity so much over the past few years that it now has almost a cult following. I have used dry flies on stillwaters ever since I began fishing them. The first reservoir trout I ever caught took a small dry Hare's Ear at Eyebrook many years ago. However, the modern development of both the patterns and the technique of fishing dry flies has unquestionably increased their effectiveness. Indeed, I would go as far as to say that nine times out of ten the use of dry flies is the best way to approach rising fish. With dry flies far less skill is needed in persuading a fish to take. If one covers a fish with a wet fly and it begins to follow, it is up to the angler to convince the fish to take. With a dry fly, on the other hand, all the angler has to do is cover the fish accurately, ensure his leader is well sunk and his flies are correctly presented and the fish will almost certainly respond.

6   Orange Seal's Fur Nymph

Hook: Kamasan B175 or 170, size 10.
Tying silk: Black.
Butt: Pearl Flashabou.
Body: Hot-orange seal's fur or substitute.
Rib: Pearl Flashabou.
Thorax: Hot-orange seal's fur or substitute covered with pheasant tail fibres.
Head: Clear varnish.

This is my top loch-style fly for catching fish near the surface. It is similar to Arthur Cove's Orange Seal's Fur Nymph, the only difference being in the pearl rib instead of the traditional gold. This is the fly I always reach for when I don't know what to put on. Perhaps that is the best accolade an angler can give a fly.

I tie it in two ways for different uses. The sinking version is tied quite sparsely on a Kamasan B175, size 10. This is an excellent point-fly for pulling when not much is showing, particularly at Grafham. The other version is a cross between a dry fly and a wake fly. It is tied with the seal's fur or substitute thickly dressed on a Kamasan B170 (fine wire), size 10. The fly is then Ginked-up and fished either static to rising fish or retrieved, when it forms a Muddler-like wake on the surface. It is lethal in both roles.

7   The Usual

Hook: Kamasan B830, size 10, leaded with fine lead-wire wrapped up and down the body.
Tying silk: Lime-green.
Tail: Olive marabou.
Body: A fifty-fifty mix of dark-olive seal's fur or substitute and fluorescent lime-green tow wool; or vary the mix to achieve different levels of brightness.
Rib: Silver wire.
Hackle: Grey partridge.
Head: Clear varnish.

This fly was originally tied to suggest a damsel nymph, and on its first outing, at Eyebrook, it accounted for fourteen trout on a day when little was caught. I thought that perhaps I had quite a good fly. Since then it has become my standard summer nymph pattern for both bank- and boat-fishing and has more than pulled its weight whenever I have used it. The beauty of the fly is that out of the water it looks like a green lure, whereas in the water it suggests the movement and colours of a damsel nymph well enough to be taken as the natural.

The naming of this fly came about in a match at Draycote. I was doing particularly well and a friend, Brian Froggatt, called over to ask what I was catching on. We had fished together many times and my reply that I was using, 'The Usual, Brian', was immediately understood. I won the match with eleven.

8   Yellow Hammer

Hook: Kamasan B175, size 10.
Tying silk: Black.
Tail: Fluorescent-yellow marabou.
Body: Fine white Sparkle chenille.
Wing: Centre wing, half-way along body, fluorescent-yellow marabou topped with pearl Flashabou, wing at head, a generous spray of fluorescent-yellow marabou.
Head: Clear varnish.

This is a mini-lure designed to conform to International rules. It is particularly good in coloured water, such as we had at Grafham for much of the 1991 season. The thinking behind the fly was to try to get as much movement and appearance of size as possible in an International size lure. The Yellow Hammer fits the bill admirably. It is a brilliant point-fly for use on a Hi-D line.

The Yellow Hammer played a large part in my success in the Pro-Am Competition at Grafham in 1991. The water was full of stock fish which seemed to be hanging round in the G-Buoy area. Despite the mountainous waves, drifting was giving consistent and rapid action, so much so that by two o'clock I had eleven fish in the boat, mostly on the Yellow Hammer.

SECRETS FROM CZECHOSLOVAKIA: SVOBODA'S RIVER FLIES

I have made good friends with many Czechoslovakian fly-fishers as we have met in European and world events over the last few years. My contact is Dr Karel, who speaks good English and has acted as interpreter in the exchange of flies, nymphs and fishing methods. Because men like Svoboda are so good on rivers, especially with grayling, I showed great interest in his patterns. In return, I filled them in on stillwater fishing. It was a fair exchange!

1   Green Hydropsyche Nymph

Hook: Long-shank size 10 weighted with lead-wire.
Tying silk: Black.
Body: Light-olive Antron mixed with a few strands of red and dubbed on.
Rib: Fine dull copper wire pulled tight to form segments; rib over shellback.
Thorax: Light-brown Antron.
Shellback: Beige/olive plastic strip.
Head: Clear varnish.

This would naturally be fished as point fly on a floating line, with perhaps a small spider pattern as a dropper. Lift a large stone from the bottom of a river and you will see just how lifelike this pattern is when you match it with a natural.

2   Grey Hydropsyche Nymph

Hook: Short-shank size 10 weighted with lead-wire.
Tying silk: Black.
Body: Grey Antron dubbed on.
Rib: Fine dull copper wire pulled tight to form segments; rib over shellback.
Thorax: Dark-brown Antron.
Shellback: Clear plastic strip.
Head: Clear varnish.

This is a colour variation of this common river insect, one of the sedge family. Fish it similarly to the previous nymph, using the rolled-nymph technique.

3 Svoboda GRHE

Hook: Short-shank, size 12, weighted with lead-wire.
Tying silk: Black.
Tail: Brown partridge hackle-fibres.
Body and thorax: Dubbed hare's ear fur.
Rib: Fine gold wire.
Shellback: A strip of clear plastic.
Head: Clear varnish.

Hare's Ear Nymphs all seem to work well no matter whose variation is used, and it is surely the most widely used pattern on rivers. This one is the simple pattern of a master fly-fisher. Put it to good use!

4 Hydropsyche Caddis Pupa

Hook: Medium-shank, size 12.
Tying silk: Black.
Body: A mixture of three parts light-olive, one part light-grey and a few strands of orange dubbed on.
Rib: A single cable strand of fine light-olive wool ribbed over shellback.
Shellback: Three strands of dark-bronze peacock herl.
Horns: Two beige paintbrush hairs.
Hackle: Sparse badger hair, spun.
Head: Clear varnish.

This is more of an emerging pattern, so watch out for caddis (sedge) hatches before you use it. A floating line, single fly, and fine leader is the approach with this one.

5 Olive Dun

Hook: Size 16.
Tying silk: Olive.
Tail: Three light-olive cock hackle-fibres.
Body: Olive tying silk.
Hackle: Sparse olive cock.
Wings: A pair of tiny grey duck breast feathers tied fanwing style.
Head: Clear varnish.

Svoboda obviously uses this little dry olive when an appropriate hatch is on. A light 8ft rod, a size 4 or 5 floating line, and a fine nylon tippet is the set up. Try wading slowly upstream and fishing a short line. You will have lots of rises and you can fish catch-and-release—but compress the hook-barb first.

6   Gold Dun

Hook: Size 16.
Tying silk: Black.
Tail: A few strands of black cock hackles.
Body: Fine gold Lurex.
Hackle: Sparse black cock.
Wing: A pair of tiny grey duck breast feathers tied fanwing style.
Head: Clear varnish.

This lovely, delicate dry fly should be fished in similar style to the olive.

---

7   Hydropsyche Caddis Adult

Hook: Size 14.
Tying silk: Dark green.
Body: Dark-green floss.
Thorax: Dubbed hare's ear.
Wing: Natural *cul de canard* feather.
Head: Clear varnish.

The fact that the Czech team did so well to win the World Championships on the Welsh Dee in 1990 demonstrates that most of their successful flies from eastern Europe also work well on British rivers. This is a dry fly to try when sedges are hatching.

---

8   Alder Fly

Hook: Size 16.
Tying silk: Olive.
Tail: Dull-green floss.
Body: One strand of black peacock herl.
Underwing: Natural *cul de canard* feather.
Overwing: Brown partridge hackle feather-fibres.
Head: Clear varnish.

Svoboda called this one Alnus Caddis, and although I am not certain of the translation, I reckon it must be an Alder. Years ago, Halford disregarded the plentiful alder fly as useless, yet other prominent fly-fishers have praised the artificial. These flies appear in great numbers in May and June, and if Svoboda thinks it is important, it must be worth a serious try.

Flies From Around the World

NEW ZEALAND

My trip to New Zealand's North Island in 1991 opened my eyes to some fabulous wild trout fishing. It was not easy fishing, but it was top-class. The England party caught many 4lb, 5lb and 6lb-plus fish, with a 7½-pounder, three 8-pounders, two 9-pounders, and one of more than 10lb to Ray Burt.

1 Red Setter

Hook: Long-shank bronze, sizes 6–8–10.
Tying silk: Black.
Tail: A generous bunch of squirrel-tail fibres.
Body: Hot-orange chenille.
Hackle: One in centre of body, one at head; long-fibred ginger cock tied sloping well back.
Head: Black or clear varnish.

I shall always remember the Red Setter because the name is that used by our New Zealand guide, Lindsay Lyons, for his business. Lindsay favours this pattern especially on a sinking fly on the lakes. He says its a good all-round pattern, but especially so late in the season as the fish begin their spawning run. It is supposed to represent two fish eggs. Its inventor was Geoff Sanderson, from Turangi.

2 Mrs Simpson

Hook: Medium-or long-shank, sizes 6–8–10.
Tying silk: Black.
Tail: Black squirrel-tail fibres.
Body: Red or yellow chenille.
Wing: Two pairs of cock pheasant rump feathers tied alongside the hook.
Head: Clear varnish.

I had often looked at this lure and thought what a ridiculous-looking pattern it was. Surely no fish would ever take it? My trip to New Zealand altered that view. First, Dennis Buck caught several fish on it, and then so did Brian Thomas. I reluctantly gave it a try on Aniwhenua Lake as a dropper—and it took two of the six fish I caught. The name came from the original Mrs Simpson for whom Edward VIII gave up his throne, the story being that this pattern would hook the 'king of the lake'. It could represent one of the small crayfish which are a main diet of trout in the Rotorua lakes.

3 Picket Fence Burglar

Hook: Medium-shank wide-gape, size 4.
Tying silk: Black.
Tail: Red wool and four black cock hackles protruding 1½ inches.
Body: A generous amount of possum hair dyed black and completely covering the hook-shank.
Head: Clear varnish.

Dennis Buck gave me this pattern. It was tied, he said, by an angler who made it famous on the stretch known as the 'picket fence' on Lake Taupo, where it accounts for many of the better fish. It could well work for big trout anywhere.

4 Dragonfly Nymph

Hook: Long-shank, sizes 8–10.
Tying silk: Black.
Tail: Tip of grey feather-fibre or biot.
Body: Black seal's fur or substitute, carrot-shaped.
Rib: Grey nymph ribbed tight.
Thorax: Black seal's fur or substitute.
Legs: Tips of grey feather-fibre or biots.
Shellback: Trimmed grey feather wing-case.
Head: Clear varnish.

One feature of New Zealand's many lakes is the large number of beautifully coloured dragonflies. These rather fearsome-looking creatures hatch from nymphs which feed on other smaller nymphs, but a trout's jaws make short work of them. Indeed, they must be easy meat for trout that can eat a 5–6-inch crayfish, claws and all.

5 New Zealand Doll

Hook: Long-shank, sizes 6–8.
Tying silk: Black.
Tail: Fluorescent-red wool.
Body: Phosphorescent white.
Hackle: A few strands of shredded white floss mixed with four strands of fine pearl Flashabou.
Back and tail top: A bunch of multi-coloured Flashabou.
Head: Black varnish.
Eyes: Yellow paint with black varnish centres.

The small fish on which trout feed heavily in New Zealand lakes are called smelt and cockabullies. I found a good number of them in the five fish we retained during our trip, fish we kept at the request of our host who wanted some for smoking. The New Zealand Doll shows that the fly I christened back in the early seventies at Ravensthorpe Reservoir—the original white Baby Doll invented by Brian Kench—has travelled well. This New Zealand Doll fly is a favourite at dusk and into darkness. The fluorescence is charged by torchlight, when the lure takes on a luminous glow which has proved deadly in attracting fish when other lures have failed.

6   Krystal Egg Fly

Hook: Short-shank wide-gape, sizes 4–6.
Tying silk: Red.
Underbody: Orange wool.
Overbody: Orange Krystal Mylar.
Hackle: Two turns of long-fibred soft white hen.
Head: Clear varnish.

The rights or wrongs of fishing fish-egg-imitating flies have long been debated. Egg-imitation flies certainly work well in Alaska, and, so it seems, in New Zealand, and not necessarily as a seasonal fly as might be expected. I include this pattern because of its record as a fish-catcher, but I wonder if it will work in Britain? I have not heard of anyone trying it.

---

7   Cicada

Hook: Medium-shank, sizes 8–10.
Tying silk: Black.
Body: Clipped natural deerhair, kept fat.
Hackle: Light-blue dun cock.
Wing: A pair of long, off-white cock hackles.
Head: Bronze peacock herl with clear varnish over normal whip-finish.

The cicada is a land-born, large-winged fly 20–30mm long. It appears from vegetation in late November, making a noise as it rubs its wings together while at rest. Once it takes flight, it often finishes up on the water, where it skitters about and makes a tasty mouthful for any trout. River fishing with an artificial is particularly exciting, and a Muddler Minnow is a good substitute pattern.

---

8   Twilight Beauty

Hook: Medium-shank down-eyed, sizes 10–12.
Tying silk: Black.
Tail: A generous bunch of bright-ginger cock hackle-fibres.
Body: Black floss built up carrot-shape.
Hackle: Bright-ginger cock.
Wings: Slips from mallard or starling primary wing feather.
Head: Clear varnish.

When we arrived in New Zealand, we were repeatedly told that if we fished the Rangataiki river, we must try a Twilight Beauty dry fly, size 10. It imitates a variety of dark mayfly which appears in late November. However, cool winds had held the hatch back, and we didn't see any of these flies until just before we left.

BELGIUM: FLIES FROM PAUL VEKEMANS

Paul Vekemans is a Belgian fly-fisher and true gentleman for whom I have the greatest respect. He has been the inspiration behind the growing interest in stillwater fly-fishing in Belgium and has represented his country at world level. Indeed, he led the Belgian team to a good bronze medal position on the Welsh Dee in 1990.

With his close friends, Christian Fouvey and Guido Vinck, he ably organizes the Belgium leg of the annual European Grand Slam Fly Fishing Championships held at a forty-acre lake outside Ghent. Paul's main skills are as a river fisherman for grayling or trout, and the change to stillwaters has come about during the last decade. Now he is fast catching up with the best in England.

This selection is mainly river flies and nymphs, with which the Belgians excel. Paul explains how to fish them.

---

1 Craddock

Hook: Sizes 10–12–14.
Tying silk: Red.
Tail: Pheasant tail fibres.
Body: Bronze peacock herl.
Rib: Medium gold flat tinsel.
Hackle: Brown partridge.
Head: Clear varnish showing red.

This nymph pattern is very good early in the season for trout or grayling. I think the fish take it for a March Brown nymph, but it does seem to be an all-round pattern. It is one to tie on when you are not too sure.

---

2 Green Thing

Hook: Long-shank, sizes 8–10.
Tying silk: Black.
Tail and body: A bunch of black with green-speckled Twinkle tied in similar style to Baby Doll.
Head: Clear varnish.

This river or lake fly is always fished on the point. Use an intermediate line and retrieve with long, slow pulls to catch lake rainbows. For river fishing use it with the across-and-down style with a small wet fly on the dropper, when it will account for browns.

3   Spectra Coachman

Hook: Sizes 18–20–22–24, down-eyed dry.
Tying silk: Black micro.
Body: Bronze peacock strand.
Hackle: Ginger cock.
Wing: A strip from Spectra sheet, tied-in figure-of-eight to achieve upright effect.
Head: Clear varnish.

The Spectra Coachman is a specialist grayling dry fly which I use for the visibility of its wings. The slightest sip-take can easily be seen even at range, and a perfectly timed strike can be made to ensure a hooked fish. It is only used on rivers or small streams, and it works well in Belgian rivers and throughout Europe.

4   Universal

Hook: Sizes 10–12–14–16–18–20–22–24, down-eyed dry.
Tying silk: Black micro.
Tail: Brown cock hackle-fibres.
Body: Grey thread with red thread rib.
Wing: Fine natural deerhair.
Hackle: Medium-brown cock.
Head: Clear varnish.

This is a general dry sedge pattern used in Belgium to imitate flies of this species, both small and large, which hatch on the rivers throughout the season. It catches brown trout or grayling. It is a favourite of mine, and I have found it very good when fished at dusk for stillwater rainbows in July and August.

5   Damsel Nymph

Hook: Long-shank, sizes 8–10, with small gold-plated brass ball head.
Tying silk: Fluorescent-green.
Tail: Olive marabou.
Body: Olive ostrich herl trimmed top and bottom.
Rib: Fine silver wire.
Hackle: Grey partridge.
Head: Prominent fluorescent-green covered with clear varnish.

I fish this nymph on a long leader on a floating line. It is a killing pattern in late June and in July and August on most lakes or gravel-pits throughout Europe.

6 Greyling

Hook: Sizes 18–20–22–24, down-eyed dry.
Tying silk: Black micro.
Body: Fine light-grey dubbing or a strand of natural heron herl.
Hackle: One or two turns of cream or light-blue dun cock.
Head: Clear varnish.

This is another simple, tiny dry fly, especially for grayling. It is important not to overdo the hackle: two turns is the maximum. A number of fish always come short when grayling dry flies have tails. It is promised that this dry fly cuts out that problem.

7 Caddis Nymph

Hook: Long-shank curved emerger type, sizes 10–12–14; weight optional.
Tying silk: Olive.
Body: Light-olive Antron dubbed and picked out with hook Velcro.
Rib: Fine copper wire.
Thorax: Dubbed grey/brown rabbit fur.
Legs: Long pheasant tail fibres.
Head: Clear varnish showing olive.

This is yet another river pattern for grayling or brown trout. It imitates the bottom-crawling caddis grub or the first stages of pupation. [*This looks such a realistic nymph that I cannot wait to try it out.—Bob Church.*]

8 Bouillon

Hook: Sizes 12–14–16.
Tying silk: Yellow.
Body: Thin grey wool tied carrot-shape.
Rib: Orange tying silk.
Hackle: Ginger cock tied well back.
Head: Built up prominently with yellow tying silk and coated with clear varnish.

This nymph was designed fifty years ago by a Belgian fisherman and is meant to imitate the sedge pupa. It is especially good for grayling in the Semois river in the south. I have included this pattern, even though it is such an old one, because I think few anglers will know about it. Also, it has stood the test of time and works on any river in Europe.

CANADA AND FRANCE

These patterns are all successful in their respective countries. They were either sent to me or given to me on my travels, and I have included them because of their past records. Each has its own little story.

Three of the Canadian flies were sent to me by Ian James, a professional fly-tyer from Ontario. I think the little buzzer nymph, in particular, is simple but excellent. The three streamer lures were sent to me to show off a new luminous plastic called Edge Bright, which forms the bodies of a series known as 'Lantern' flies. They certainly shine brightly.

---

1 Canadian Lure

Hook: Long-shank, sizes 8–10.
Tying silk: Black.
Body: Silver Mylar tinsel.
Underwing: Black hair, goat or bucktail.
Overwing: Green peacock herl from the sword feather.
Head: Black varnish.

Ian's first pattern is a fishy lure that is much like our British designs—shades of the old Alexandra! I assume we should fish this similarly, with various sinking-line techniques.

---

2 Copper Buzzer

Hook: Sizes 12–14.
Tying silk: Black or orange.
Body: Tightly coiled fine copper wire.
Thorax: Hot-orange seal's fur or substitute.
Breather: White floss.
Head: Clear varnish.

Ian James' Canadian buzzer pattern incorporates the same effective orange colour as the English nymph. However, his simple copper-wire body gives the nymph considerable weight while remaining a delicate, slim-bodied pattern. It is very good when you want to fish delicately but deep. Different colours can be used with the fine copper-wire body.

3 Canadian Caddis

Hook: Sizes 12–14.
Tying silk: Black.
Body: Orange seal's fur or substitute.
Rib: Tying silk.
Hackle: Long-fibred soft black hen hackle.
Thorax: Black ostrich herl.
Head: Clear varnish.

This unusual leggy caddis pattern really caught my eye because a hatching sedge pupa does look a tangled mess of legs and antennae. The long, soft, spidery hackle-fibres imitate it perfectly. Fish the fly close to the surface with a slow retrieve. This is another Ian James' pattern.

4 Yellow Dean River Lantern

Hook: Sizes 4–6–8 salmon singles.
Tying silk: Black.
Tail: Black squirrel-tail hair as long as the hook-shank.
Underbody: Flat silver tinsel.
Overbody: Fluorescent-yellow Edge Bright.
Hackle: A full long-fibred saddle-hackle dyed fluorescent yellow. The hackle-fibres should reach just short of the hook-point.
Head: Black varnish.

Rob Wagoner first used Edge Bright for covering the bodies of steelhead flies known as the Dean River Lanterns. These were used with excellent results on the famous Dean River in British Columbia. To use Edge Bright, cut ⅛-inch strips with a Stanley knife and straight metal edge. The material comes in all the usual bright colours.

5 Orange Steelhead Charlie

Hook: Sizes 4–6–8 salmon singles.
Tying silk: White.
Underbody: Flat silver tinsel.
Eyes: Chain beads.
Overbody: Fluorescent-orange Edge Bright.
Underwing: Squirrel-tail hair dyed orange and tied in as a throat hackle for the full length of hook.
Head: Clear varnish.

Steelhead Charlie is another Rob Wagoner pattern. It is used for fishing deep to slow-moving fish lying in large pools and catches rainbows in our big still-waters.

6 Lac de Landie Nymph

Hook: Sizes 10–12.
Tying silk: Black.
Tail: Natural squirrel-tail hair.
Body: Red Power Gum elastic; substitute, Nymph Glass.
Thorax: Bronze peacock herl.
Wing: A pair of brown goose biots tied as two cheeks.
Head: White suspender ball. Clear varnish.

I had the time of my life when I visited Lac de Landie, a lovely high-altitude lake on the Plateau d'Artense, close to Clermont Ferrand in France. The fishing was brilliant, the food unbeatable, and the people so friendly. The fishery manager gave me this floating nymph, which, he said, catches him lots of trout.

7 Polar Shrimp

Hook: Sizes 4–6–8 salmon singles.
Tying silk: Black.
Tail: Long cock hackle-fibres dyed fluorescent red.
Underbody: Flat silver tinsel.
Overbody: Fluorescent-red Edge Bright.
Hackle: Saddle hackle dyed fluorescent red.
Wing: White soft hair; goat, bucktail.
Head: Black varnish.

The last of the Lantern flies, this one is tied similarly to the general streamer lure design, but has the 'magic' shining body. It is a superb steelhead pattern, but is good also for all salmon and other game species encountered in Canada and Alaska.

8 Guillot's Special

Hook: Sizes 10–12 with a small lead-shot pinched-and-glued behind the eye.
Tying silk: Black.
Tail: A bunch of red marabou topped with a few strands of pearl Crystal.
Body: Green Bobbydazzlelure.
Wing: Black marabou.
Cheeks: Strips of copper Lurex.
Head: Black varnish.

Jean Guillot is a pioneer of the new-found sport of reservoir trout fishing in France. He has been successful with good catches in competitions and this attractor pattern is one of his best inventions.

CZECHOSLOVAKIAN RIVER FLIES

I made good friends with the Czechoslovakian International fly-fishing team when they became World Champions on the Welsh Dee in 1990, but we were limited to sign language. They are good river fishermen and excel at grayling and trout, but their great wish was to learn more about stillwater trout fishing. I fished the stillwater day on Llyn Brenig with one of their team, Gerry. It was a hard day, and because I managed five fish to finish second, and Gerry caught one, he thought I was some sort of genius! We exchanged flies and he gave me a collection of river patterns. Those which are heavily leaded are grouped elsewhere.

---

1 Olive Deerhair Sedge

Hook: Sizes 12–14.
Tying silk: Black.
Tail: Yellow floss kept short.
Body: Olive floss.
Wing: Fine-fibred natural deerhair.
Hackle: Medium-brown cock.
Head: Clear varnish.

This buoyant dry sedge pattern should fish well in fast, streamy water. In Britain it should float well without being dragged under by turbulence.

---

2 Pale Deerhair Sedge

Hook: Sizes 12–14.
Tying silk: Fawn.
Tail: Olive floss kept short.
Body: Fawn or beige floss.
Wing: Light, fine-fibred natural deerhair.
Hackle: One turn of light-brown cock.
Head: Clear varnish.

This sedge is similar to the previous one, but lighter in colour and dressing. It is best fished dry in a steady flow.

3 Beige Sedge Pupa

Hook: Sizes 12–14, lightly leaded if wished.
Tying silk: Black.
Body: Beige Antron dubbed on.
Shellback: Long strands of beige Antron tied in loosely.
Thorax: Single strand of bronze peacock herl.
Head: Clear varnish.

This Sedge Pupa can be fished just sub-surface when a hatch is on. Alternatively, the lightly weighted version can be used on a floating line and a sinking braided leader.

---

4 March Brown Spider Variant

Hook: Size 12.
Tying silk: Brown.
Tail: Brown partridge hackle feather-fibres.
Body: Light-brown seal's fur or substitute.
Rib: Fine gold tinsel.
Hackle: Brown partridge.
Head: Clear varnish.

This pattern should be fished across and down as a wet fly on a floating or sink-tip line and braided leader, similar to the Yorkshire river style. It fishes well when the water is up a little.

---

5 Shrimp

Hook: Curved type, lightly weighted size 12.
Tying silk: Black.
Underbody: Beige or honey Antron.
Underbody rib: Red floss.
Shellback: Brown raffia, varnished.
Shellback rib: Clear nylon, about 3lb breaking strain.
Head: Clear varnish.

Like all shrimp patterns, this one should be fished deep, drifting at the same speed as the flow. Upstream and dead-drift methods are good, but the east European rolled-nymph method might be even better.

6 Tiny Beetle

Hook: Sizes 16–18.
Tying silk: Green.
Tail: Phosphorescent white Flashabou.
Body: Bronze peacock herl.
Hackle: Grizzle cock.
Head: Clear varnish.

Tiny dark beetles are common in all European countries, and in high summer they are blown on to the water, where keen-eyed trout soon become aware of the opportunity presented and begin to feed on them. It pays to have a good imitation ready.

7 Pale-winged Olive

Hook: Sizes 16–18.
Tying silk: Olive.
Tail: White cock hackle-fibres.
Body: Olive tying silk, varnished.
Wing: Pale starling tied upright.
Hackle: Light blue-dun.
Head: Clear varnish.

This is a good, delicate dry fly for those magical hatches of tiny light-winged olives. It needs to be cast accurately on ultra-light tackle and leader to achieve perfect upstream presentation. Cover the continuous riser only, letting the fly travel a metre or so before re-casting. Accuracy is vital. An olive hatch comes on quickly and is gone just as quickly, especially in cold conditions. The advice is to change as soon as you see those first olives sail past.

8 Blue-dun Variant

Hook: Size 16.
Tying silk: Black.
Tail: Grizzle hackle-fibres.
Body: Grey heron herl.
Rib: Primrose tying silk.
Wing: A pair of trimmed off-white cock hackles tied upright.
Hackle: Grizzle cock.
Head: Clear varnish.

This represents a common fly well distributed throughout Europe, with the artificial used on most rivers which hold wild trout and grayling. The variant is worth tying and trying alongside more traditional patterns.

FINLAND

Finland was the only place I have visited for a fishing holiday where I lost weight. I just couldn't get used to the idea of eating reindeer meat at every meal, and as the alternative was raw fish, I went on a self-imposed diet. The temperature was well in the 80s Fahrenheit and I was doing a lot of walking in chest-waders. After two weeks I was super-fit and had caught my largest wild river brown trout, a lovely fish of 7lb 6oz, on a small nymph.

Our fishing was in the north of the country, on the borders of Lapland and Russia. The rivers Kitka and Kuusinki, ran through lakes, and I found the inflows and outflows great places to fish for many different species.

As well as the brown trout and grayling, the prized whitefish provided great sport.

---

1 Jardine's Wiggle Hare's Ear

Hook: Leaded curved grub or shrimp hook, sizes 10–12.
Tying silk: Black.
Tail: Olive marabou.
Body: Dubbed hare's ear.
Rib: Copper wire.
Head: Clear varnish.

Charles Jardine sent me a batch of weighted nymphs and dry flies before I went to Finland, confident that some would be of use. I shall be forever in his debt, for this pattern produced a magnificent brown of 7lb 6oz. I hooked it on light tackle in a fast, shallow run while I was up to my waist in the centre of the river and without a net.

The fish's first leap was a magnificent four-footer, and I thought I would never land the fish. I slowly edged back to the bank and had had the fish on for 15 minutes when it leapt again as it raced into only one foot of water, fell back and stunned itself on the rocky bottom. I leapt on the fish without ceremony and pushed it up on to the grassy bank. I was overjoyed, and it was the only fish I kept out of more than 200 during the two weeks. Thanks, Charles! I am sure it was the wiggle action of the tail that did the trick!.

---

2 Juha's Sedge Pupa

Hook: Curved emerger type, leaded, sizes 8–10.
Tying silk: Green.
Body: Green and grey Antron dubbing mix.
Rib: Gold oval thread.
Thorax: Hare's ear fur.
Legs: Speckled feather-fibre, substitute cock pheasant tail feather-fibres, tied at throat.
Head: Clear varnish.

I watched as Juha fished his way down a deep run on the Kuusinki river. It was around midday, and we expected little in the way of sport. He was using a floating line and this single, weighted Sedge Pupa. He hooked a fish in a featureless stretch and soon we both realized it was big. The fight was more dogged than spectacular, and the fish turned out to be a brown of 8½lb. This nymph also caught many grayling and smaller browns. Back home this nymph has done well for me on rivers and stillwaters.

The brown trout that begin life in these two Finnish rivers migrate downstream after two years, crossing the Russian border and moving into a lake called Paanajarvi. Here they grow as a sea-trout would at sea. Scale-readings have shown that some fish had been back to spawn four times.

3 Brown Bear Dry Fly

Hook: Wide-gape size 8.
Tying silk: Black.
Body: Dubbing mix of brown, yellow and olive seal's fur or substitute.
Rib: Fine gold oval thread.
Hackle: Light ginger, palmered.
Wing: Two bunches of brown bear hair or substitute.
Head hackle: Dark ginger cock tied generously.
Head: Clear varnish.

This dry fly was given to me by our Finnish guide, Juha Vaino. It was for use in the fast, turbulent rapids, which are so rough that normal dry flies are just sucked under. This pattern rides high and is virtually unsinkable. As we walked down the river, Juha pointed out 'bear scratching' areas, where a fallen tree's broken stubby branches would be covered in bear hair. Alas, we didn't see a bear—just reindeer, more reindeer, and the most ferocious biting mosquitoes I have ever come across.

4 Moser's Goldhead Nymph

Hook: Partridge International medium-weight, sizes 10–12, with an appropriate-sized gold-plated brass ball threaded on to the hook to stop at the eye.
Tying silk: Black. Secure the brass ball by whipping behind it.
Body: Dubbing mix of two parts grey and one part brown Antron with a few particles of pearl Krystal, left rough and bulky. Other colours can be tried.
Head: Clear varnish.

Roman Moser, the well-known Austrian fly-fisher and fly-tyer, introduced the gold ball idea a few years ago. Now many different patterns exist for both rivers and stillwaters. This one began life as a river nymph and is bounced along the bottom by the current as it is fished on a floating line. Strike indicators are often used to detect takes when these nymphs are fished in fast water.

5 Ogborne's Fluorescent Stick-fly

Hook: Tinhead, size 10, with head painted fluorescent green.
Tying silk: Black.
Tag: Fluorescent-green Flashabou.
Body: Bronze peacock herl.
Rib: Copper wire.
Head: Clear varnish.

Bright green is quite common in aquatic insects, and Chris Ogborne tied this variation of the Stick-fly as an experiment. It caught a number of mixed fish for him and me on both the Kitka and Kuusinki rivers. Fish it on a floating or sink-tip line and a weighted braided leader.

6 Canning's Sight Fly

Hook: Size 10.
Tying silk: Olive.
Body: Light-olive seal's fur or substitute.
Thorax: Dark-olive seal's fur or substitute.
Hackle: Grizzle cock tied parachute-style on to a twist of medium-thick copper wire which acts as a base.
Sight indicator: Fluorescent-red yarn tied on to a twist of medium-thick copper wire which acts as a base.
Head: Clear varnish.

Paul Canning is one of the best tactical fly-fishers I know, and he invented this fly for the fast, turbulent rapids of the Finnish rivers. He built the sight-indicator into the fly rather than have it at the end of the line—a great idea!

7 Church's River Caddis

Hook: Long-shank Tinhead, sizes 10–12, with head painted yellow. Extra weight can be added if needed.
Tying silk: Black.
Tail: Brown rabbit fur fibres.
Body: Dubbed brown rabbit fur.
Hackle: Brown partridge.
Head: Clear varnish.

I have found the best style of using this large nymph is to fish it dead-drift with a floating line. You cast across and well upstream, and keep in touch by re-trieving slack line as the nymph drifts back, passes your position and continues downstream. The nymph travels at exactly the same speed as the current, and you can pay out line as it goes down. Keep a careful watch on the fly-line tip, which will register a take. I caught many grayling and trout like this, and the method works on all rivers when this nymph is used.

8 Ure Caddis

Hook: Size 10.
Tying silk: Black.
Eyes: A pair of substitute lead-shot pinched on to 4lb nylon and tied into an eye position. This Van Klinken idea of weighting a fly has been bettered by the little dumbbell weights which are now available.
Tail: A strand of creamy-yellow wool with end burned.
Feelers: Partridge hackle tied around the wool.
Body: Dubbed hare's ear and mole mixed.
Head: Clear varnish.

This fly was given to me by that great fly-fisher, Oliver Edwards, when I spent a weekend on his local river Ure. The weighting idea comes from the continent, but Oliver's addition of the burnt-wool caddis grub head was, in my opinion, the making of the nymph's success. Fish it at point on a floating or sink-tip line, with a small spider pattern about two feet above it. The technique worked well on the Finnish rivers.

SPAIN

Many people think of Spain as somewhere to go for a holiday in the sun, but British anglers go there for the excellent carp and catfish fishing, and for trout and salmon fishing in the north-west. My own fishing there was on some of the best game fish rivers of the north and central regions, Sella, Narcia and Tormes.

On my travels I met up with the two Rafaels: Rafael Madriago, who speaks good English, and Rafael del Pozo, who speaks no English. Both are fanatical river fly-fishers, and Rafael del Pozo is one of the best and most inventive fly-tyers I have met. He has written a classic book on entomology called *Moscas Para La Pesca*.

Spanish fly-tyers use special hackle feathers, which come from a cockerel known as the 'cock of Leon'. These have the stiffest hackle-fibres of any bird.

---

1 Upside-down Dry Sedge

Hook: Long-shank, size 12.
Tying silk: Brown.
Tail: Fawn *cul-de-canard* feather-fibres.
Body: A dubbing mix of amber seal's fur or substitute and a few strands of dark-brown *cul-de-canard* feather stems pre-stripped to leave just the fine quills.
Thorax: Built up of the body dubbing mix.
Wing: A synthetic wing of quite stiff lace-like material tied in beneath the hook-shank. Hen pheasant wing feather-fibres coated with clear varnish and allowed to dry will serve as a substitute.
Head: Clear varnish.

Rafael gave me a lot of these dry sedge flies, and they have been superb not only on rivers but on English reservoirs and Irish loughs. This fly floats upside-down with the hook-bend and point well hidden from the trout's vision. Once you have mastered the tying technique, you can devise your own colour schemes to match the sedges which hatch on your water. The fly is especially good for evening fishing, when it will tempt larger-than-average fish.

---

2 Flat Nymph

Hook: Sizes 10–12 specially leaded with two or three double layers of pear-shaped lead cut from a wine-bottle top.
Tying silk: Brown.
Tail: Six fibres of cock-of-Leon hackle, or a best light grizzle as substitute.
Body: Grey floss, extended to cover lead thorax.
Gills: Three each side of the tiniest dark-brown cock hackle-tips you can find—those normally ignored at the tip of the capes are ideal.
Legs: Six legs, three each side, of knotted cock-of-Leon hackle-fibres.
Shellback and head extension: Cock-of-Leon hackle or substitute tied in to cover the back of the thorax. Trap it with tying silk behind the hook-eye and trim to shape to form the head extension. Paint thorax, head and legs with clear Copydex.
Eyes: Blobs of red varnish.

The Flat Nymph is Rafael Madriago's favourite on rivers such as the Tormes when fish are lying deep because no hatch is on. It is a delicate weighted pattern which imitates many aquatic nymphs (olives), and I have used it successfully on all the rivers where I have tried it. A plus-point for this nymph is that it can be used more safely with a light leader than can other heavily leaded nymphs.

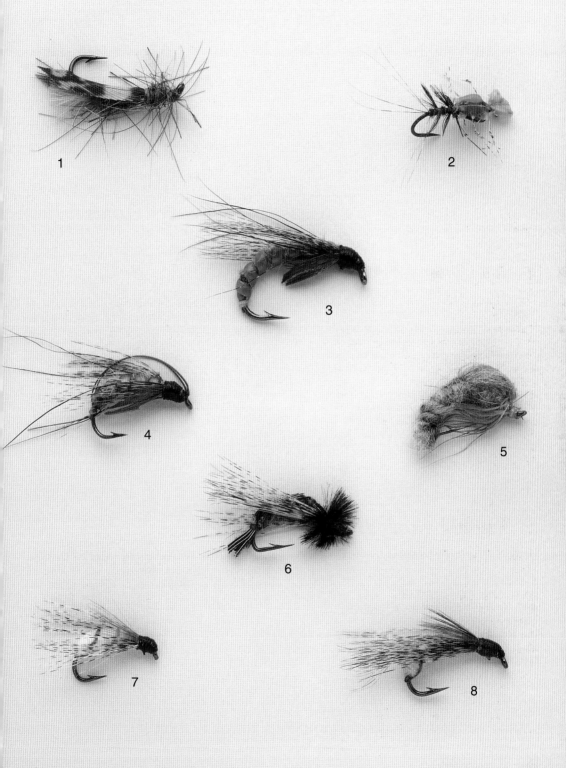

3 Olive Sedge Pupa

Hook: Curved-style; can be lightly weighted. Sizes 8–10–12.
Tying silk: Black.
Tag: Olive silk right round hook-bend.
Body: Light-olive Antron or seal's fur or substitute.
Rib: Wide olive Swanandaze or olive Nymph Glass.
Legs (cheeks): Slips of grey feather-fibre.
Wing: A slip of cock-of-Leon hackle-fibres down each flank.
Head: Clear or black varnish.

This Olive Sedge Pupa pattern and the Light Brown Sedge Pupa which follows are brilliant imitations of the naturals and are flies for the summer months. Rafael del Pozo designed these nymphs for rivers, but they have been proved quite deadly on still-waters all over Europe.

4 Light-brown Sedge Pupa

Hook: Curved style; can be lightly weighted. Sizes 8–10–12.
Tying silk: Black.
Tag: Olive silk right round hook-bend.
Body: Brown Antron or seal's fur or substitute.
Rib: Wide light-brown Swanandaze or brown Nymph Glass.
Legs (cheeks): Slips of grey feather-fibre.
Wing: A slip of cock-of-Leon hackle-fibres down each flank.
Antennae: One pair of brown hackle stalks (optional).
Head: Clear or black varnish.

The optional pair of antennae are first tied in at the tail, and then tied in again at the head when the dressing is finished off.

5 Antron Emerging Sedge

Hook: Special hump-backed sedge hook, sizes 10–12.
Tying silk: Beige.
Body: Greyish-brown Antron begun well round hook-bend and kept uneven and scruffy.
Thorax: Body Antron built up.
Hackle: Two turns of light-brown hen with top fibres torn off.
Head: Clear varnish.

Rafael deliberately kept this emerging Sedge Pupa rough and scruffy, because that is exactly how the natural looks—a tangled mass of legs, wings and antennae.

6   Dark Sedge Pupa

Hook: Special hump-backed sedge hook, sizes 10–12.
Tying silk: Black.
Tail and back: Eight stripped strands of black ostrich herl.
Body: Grey Antron.
Rib: Thick brown thread.
Hackle: Black ostrich herl.
Wing: A few strands of cock-of-Leon hackle-fibres down each flank.
Head: Clear varnish.

The sedges on some rivers and Scottish lochs I have fished have been very dark, even black, and this Dark Sedge Pupa imitates them well. Fish it just sub-surface when fish are rising.

7   White Sedge Pupa

Hook: Curved sedge hook, sizes 12–14.
Tying silk: Black.
Body: White wool tied fat.
Rib: Brown thread.
Wing: Cock-of-Leon hackle-fibres down each flank.
Head: Clear or black varnish.

This White Sedge Pupa has proved the best pattern for English lakes and reservoirs. I am not sure where Rafael intended it to be used, but it has done well at Grafham and Rutland Water.

8   Yellow-and-brown Pupa

Hook: Curved sedge hook, sizes 10–12.
Tying silk: Black.
Body: Rear one-third, yellow wool; front two-thirds, light-brown.
Rib: Dark-brown thread.
Upper wing: A bunch of light-brown hackle-fibres.
Wing: Long cock-of-Leon hackle-fibres down each flank, tied in a little down the body to expose a short section of brown wool which must be clear varnished.
Head: Clear varnish.

This colour scheme has long been a favourite of mine for my own sedge pupae patterns, but Rafael's pattern has more detail which means that it should 'produce' better. I feel it will be a good all-round pattern, and I look forward to trying it.

SWEDEN

Who better to put together a Swedish collection than Thomas Tykosson, who comes from the Umea region, where the sea-trout fishing is excellent. Thomas fishes all over Sweden for sea-trout, salmon, grayling, trout and char, and if ever he feels like a change, he pops over the border into Norway. Scandinavia's wealth of game-fishing gives him every opportunity to catch big fish regularly.

I am convinced that many flies from around the world will catch trout in the UK, just as whenever I have fished abroad, my English flies have often worked better than local favourites.

---

1 Gronlund's Nattslanda (Gronlund's Sedge)

Hook: Mustad 94831, sizes 12–14.
Tying silk: Black.
Tail: A few white cock fibres.
Body: Brown latex.
Wing: Brown mallard, natural or dyed.
Hackle: Brown cock, quite heavily hackled.
Head: Clear varnish.

This pattern was devised by Sven Gronlund. When night fishing in northern Sweden he often heard splashes from fish taking the quite large dark-brown sedge-flies that were jumping and skating on the surface. This imitation serves as a good general imitation of the often large dark sedges that are important food items for grayling, brown trout and Arctic char in our part of the country. It is best fished not static, but with small pulls to make it more living. It really does have the right overall appearance to make large fish rise from the depths to grab it. The take is often hard and decisive.

---

2 Deep Purple

Hook: Standard wet-fly, sizes 10–12–14.
Tying silk: Purple.
Body: Purple silk floss.
Hackle: Purple cock, palmered.
Wings: Purple duck.
Head: Clear varnish.

Another fly from the same company, Gronlunds'; this pattern is tied on both doubles and as a dry fish, but it works best as a wet, as shown. Sven Gronlund's father, Reinhold Gronlund, used to go fishing from a boat in the mountains and often heard people talk about an all-purple fly that worked well. He was a good fly-dresser and later made it up, and it has since become a well-known fly. Although it's not an imitative pattern, it still works well on all northern game fish. No one knows how old it is, but we must give Reinhold credit for its popularity. It has been responsible for many big fish in northern Sweden.

3 Rackelhanen

Hook: Standard dry, size 12.
Tying silk: Brown.
Body: Brown poly-yarn, clipped and dubbed.
Wings: Brown poly-yarn.
Head: Clear varnish.

This fly was made up by Kennet Bostrom to represent a small sedge fly. It is interesting in that the whole fly consists of only one material, and it is easy to tie. It has no hackle and floats low in the water. When it is treated with a good flotant, it can be pulled below the surface and then it bobs up again like a cork. This action is sometime effective in inducing a trout to take.

4 Bjork Masken (Birch Worm)

Hook: Standard wet, size 12.
Tying silk: Black.
Body: Dark olive-green dubbing.
Back and tail: Light olive-green fibres.
Head: Clear varnish.

This fly is tied backwards. You must fix the thread at the hook-bend and tie it back to the eye. Tie in the fibres pointing forward, and then dub the body back to the bend. Take the fibres, slope them backwards on the back of the fly, and tie in. Make a whip-finish at the bend.

The birch is a common tree in Sweden, growing along many streams, and it is from this tree that this insect falls into the water. Fish seem very fond of it. The fly is best fished on a free drift with a bite-indicator on the leader.

5 Superpuppan (Super Pupa)

Hook: Wet, size 12.
Tying silk: Black.
Body: Rear two-thirds, Fly-Rite No. 9 (golden-yellow); front one-third, 60 per cent Fly-Rite No. 2, and 40 per cent No. 26, making a dark-dun colour.
Hackle: A good-quality dark-blue dun, palmered and then clipped, leaving just the fibres on the side. The hackle should form a slight V-shape on each side.
Head: Clear varnish.

This pattern comes from the well-known fly-tyer Lennart Bergqvist. It may be fished dry or wet just below the surface. It represents a hatching sedge and is a real killer, since sedge flies are very important in Sweden's fishing. We have between 200 and 300 different sedge species in Sweden and, in their different stages, they are important food items for fish during most of the season. The Super Pupa is not a true-to-life imitation of a hatching sedge, but its shape and hackle trigger the right reactions from trout and grayling. Different colour variations are used from place to place, but the one given is the most common. You can, of course, use your own dubbing instead of Fly-Rite.

6 Monsterpuppan (Monster Pupa)

Hook: Long-shank, sizes 10–12.
Tying silk: Yellow.
Body: Light-brown rabbit or hare. Use a dubbing loop and plenty of material.
Thorax: Dark-brown rabbit or hare.
Head: Clear varnish.

I have been given this pattern by Torsten Johansson, who lives in Bergslagen, a part of Sweden that is frequently visited by anglers from elsewhere. Much of the fishing is in lakes in which both rainbows and browns are stocked, and they have hatches of really big sedges, 4–5cm, in September and October. This pattern represents a sedge both hatching and egg-laying. It should be fished well greased and both static and with short pulls. It works from July until the season's end. Pick out the body with hooked Velcro before you use this one.

7 Getingen (Wasp)

Hook: Size 12, down-eyed.
Tying silk: Black.
Body: A small round piece of balsa carved to the right shape and with a small central cut lengthways on the down side so that the wood can be Super-glued to the hook-shank. Paint the whole body a light golden-brown, leave it to dry, and then paint on the black sections.
Hackle: Furnace. As a last step, add two or three turns of furnace cock at the head and whip-finish.
Head: Clear varnish.

This is one of Rolf Ahlkvist's creations. During autumn, when the air is cooling, terrestrial insects become more important. Wasps are getting dull, and on some days they may be seen drifting with the wind and landing on the water. Wasps must give the fish a good deal of energy because they are keen to take them, the last big insects available before winter. This is also the time of year when big, normally fry-feeding browns will rise to fly. Rolf's pattern uses balsawood, which makes it durable and buoyant. It's a little tedious to make, but well worth while. The shape of the wasp does not have to be imitated. The black/yellow pattern and the size seem to be the triggers.

8 Gul Forsslanda (Yellow Stream Mayfly)

Hook: Mustad 94833, size 12.
Tying silk: Yellow.
Tail: Ginger cock hackle-fibres the same length as the hook.
Body: Dubbed Fly-Rite No. 9 (golden-yellow).
Hackle: Light ginger, tied conventionally but then separated with the tying thread beneath the hook to form a wide V.
Wings: Light-dun hen saddle burned with Sunrise wingburner.
Head: Clear varnish.

This is one of many mayflies (*Heptagenia sulphurea*) described by Lennart Berqvist in his book *Fly Tying My Way*. Mayflies aren't that important in northern Sweden, which is the most important area if you wish to fish for wild browns, char and grayling in streams. However, we do have hatches of mayflies about the last week of June, and since fish are keen to take them, you should have a few imitations, both adults and pupae, in your fly-box. This is one of my personal favourites. Its light colour makes it visible at long distances and it is fairly easy to tie compared to many patterns that seem to have been created for the benefit of fly-tyers rather than the fish.

TASMANIAN LAKES

A three-week fishing trip to the central Tasmanian plateau will forever stay clear in my memory. It was quite an adventure, and the remote gum tree forests and wild-life were worth going to see on their own. The fishing was good, but difficult on some waters and easy on others. The World Championship was fished on Bronte Lake, Little Pine Lagoon and London Lakes, but because of our continuous practice fishing, the fish became more wary as the championship approached.

Our guide was the genial Noel Jetson, a real countryman who could rustle up a hot meal miles from anywhere. He even persuaded me to eat freshly caught and greenwood-smoked trout. His favourite fishing method was dry-fly fishing in the weedy shallows, but this failed for both him and the English team in practice.

---

1 Brian's Fiery Sedge

Hook: Kamasan B175, sizes 10–12.
Tying silk: Yellow.
Tail: Rusty fiery-brown cock hackle tied palmer style.
Rib: Gold Lurex.
Wing: Teal feather-fibre slips.
Head: Clear varnish.

This is one of the flies that helped win the World Championship for the English team in Tasmania. The unusually-coloured cock cape, a rusty-fiery-brown, was dyed for Brian Thomas by Vera Dyson, and what a winner it was! The various sedge flies tied from its feathers by all team members caught most of the trout during the championship, and, indeed, during the whole three weeks we were there. We all had the greatest faith in this fly on all three waters, and in the end, John Pawson came first, Brian Thomas was second, I was fourth, Brian Leadbetter twelfth and Dennis Buck thirteenth—a brilliant team performance on the other side of the world! Fish it on a floating line in the surface film and with a steady retrieve.

---

2 White-winged Wickham's

Hook: Sizes 10–12.
Tying silk: Black.
Tail: Dark ginger cock hackle-fibres.
Body: Gold tinsel.
Rib: Fine silver wire.
Hackle: Palmer-style dark-ginger cock hackle.
Wing: Light silver-grey, almost white, feather-fibre slips.
Head: Clear varnish.

The Wickham's Fancy, in all its forms, is always one of my favourite flies once a few sedges are about. Walking through the dry rushes at Bronte Lake, I disturbed lots of resting silverhorn sedges, but we had all been so filled with theory and local methods before travelling to Tasmania, I for one had never considered taking Wickham's Fancy wet flies. However, I did have my fly-tying kit, and soon I had a small stock to try out along with Brian's Fiery Brown. The feather used for the wing was lighter than normal, but I could not choose between these two flies. Noel Jetson, our guide, was impressed. 'I'm supposed to be showing you lot how to fish my lakes', he said, 'but it's you who are showing me!'

3 Highland Dun

Hook: Size 12, up-eyed.
Tying silk: Black.
Tail: Grey partridge hackle-fibres.
Body: Grey rabbit fur dubbed on.
Rib: Fine gold oval thread.
Hackle: Long fibred grey partridge.
Wing: Greyish-brown feather-fibre.
Head: Clear varnish.

The Highland Dun is Tasmania's Mayfly, and it appears in good numbers during late November and early December. It is a large-enough tasty morsel to bring the fish up. However, because of continuous wind and rain, the season for this fly was only just beginning when it was time to leave, and I managed only a couple of sessions when the natural was hatching.

4 Brown Tadpole

Hook: Partridge Captain Hamilton heavyweight, size 10.
Tying silk: Black.
Tail: Light ginger-red fox fur.
Body: Dark-brown fur dubbed on.
Rib: Tying silk.
Head: Clear varnish.

The shallow, weedy margins of all the lakes we fished were teeming with tiny frogs which croaked noisily as dusk approached. These just had to be part of the trout's food chain, hence this simple imitation. It was given to me by Alun Jones, a member of the Welsh team.

5 Red-backed Gum Beetle

Hook: Sizes 10–12.
Tying silk: Black.
Body: A piece of shaped and split cork, stuck on to the top of the hook-shank and painted red.
Hackle: Dark-brown hen hackle-fibres.
Head: Clear varnish.

The whole of the central Tasmanian plateau is covered in dense forest, with the eucalyptus or gum the dominant tree. On the leaves, we found the red gum beetle and a yellow-backed variety. Both blew on to the lakes in large numbers, and the trout fed well on them, being sometimes completely preoccupied. A fish taken on one such day at Dee Lake and kept for the barbecue had more than fifty beetles in its stomach.

6   Yellow-backed Gum Beetle

Hook: Size 12.
Tying silk: Black.
Body: Amber and brown Antron, mixed and dubbed on.
Hackle: Greenwell's hen.
Shellback: A strip of plastic foam coloured yellow with a Pantone pen.
Head: Clear varnish.

The yellow-backed gum beetle was perhaps more common than the red-backed. I remember wading well out from the downwind shore of Bronte Lake and having the top of my chest-waders covered in both types of beetle that had drifted right across the lake. We had a good catch that evening, with fish taken right off the top. As we never killed any, I cannot be sure of their stomach content, but my guess is that they were full of gum beetles.

7   Spent Black Gnat

Hook: Size 12, up-eyed.
Tying silk: Black.
Tail: Black hackle-fibres.
Body: Black seal's fur or substitute.
Rib: Fine silver wire.
Hackle: Black cock.
Wing: White polypropylene, tied spent.
Head: Clear varnish.

One of our favourite spots for practice was Brady's Lake, only a few miles from our base camp. The fish, both rainbows and browns, were plentiful and rose well during the evening. The Tasmanian Mayfly (*Atalophle bioides*) is nothing like our European fly, being smaller and darker. The evening fishing—casting to rises—was to this spent fly returning to the water to lay eggs and die.

8   Tasmanian Caenis

Hook: Sizes 12–14.
Tying silk: White.
Tail: White cock hackle-fibres.
Body: White seal's fur or substitute.
Hackle: Palmer style. Rear half, white cock; front half, badger cock.
Head: Clear varnish.

On three or four occasions I was at the lakeside for first light, 4 am, which is when the tailing trout come right into the margins to feed, sometimes in water so shallow that their bellies are touching bottom and their backs are sticking out of the water. This is a feeding behaviour I have never encountered anywhere else. I had to keep very quiet, casting from well back on the bank, but using short, accurate casts with a dry fly. Noel would use his Red Tag, but after I had failed several times with that, I began to use either the Black Spent or this Caenis. I caught three trout one morning and lost two larger fish on this pattern on Bronte Lake.

AMERICA

I asked my good friend Barry Unwin, of Fulling Mill Flies, to come up with eight winners from America. Barry's father, Colonel Andy Unwin, started their fly-tying business twenty-five years ago at Nandi Hills, Kenya. Since then, as well as supplying flies to all game-fishing countries, Barry has specialized in the best American patterns. I well remember the set of size 26 dry flies which he supplied to the England World Team in 1990, and I shall never forget catching some lovely grayling on the Welsh Dee on his Adams and Light Cahill. I had never before fished so fine with such tiny flies.

Barry said that selecting just eight flies for the whole of the United States was difficult with so many popular patterns to choose from. Instead, he picked the eight most popular flies that Fulling Mill offers its customers in the USA.

1 Adams

Hook: Scorpion 31180 all-purpose lightweight, sizes 10–12–14–16–18–20–22–24–26–28.
Tying silk: Grey.
Tail: Grizzle and brown hackle-fibres mixed.
Body: Kenya mole, muskrat or dark-dun synthetic equivalent.
Wing: Grizzle hackle-tips.
Hackle: Grizzle and brown cock mixed.

To go fishing on certain waters without this fly, probably one of the most successful patterns of all time, would be folly. The variety of dressings spawned from Len Halliday's original spentwing dressing are legion. First used on the Boardman River in 1922, it is now popularly tied in the upwing version shown. Other variations include the Irresistibles, Thorax patterns, Parachutes, Wulffs, Humpies, and, more recently, the new *cul-de-canard* versions. It can be equally effective as a winged wet fly or nymph, and has been successful for me in rivers as diverse as the Gallatin in Montana, the Mathioya in Kenya, and our own Test and Itchen. The most memorable fish I recall taking on it was a lovely 3½lb brownie from the Test at Timsbury on a size 28.

2 Elkhair Caddis Tan

Hook: Scorpion 31180 all-purpose lightweight or 31550 all-purpose medium, sizes 12–14–16–18–20–22–24.
Tying silk: Brown, tan or white.
Body: Light-tan hare's fur or synthetic dubbing.
Rib: Fine copper wire reversed through hackle.
Hackle: Ginger cock palmered over body.
Wing: Light elkhair tied on top of the hook with several fibres extending along the side and the butt of the elkhair extended forward to form the head.
Head: Clear varnish.

Another modern classic, this pattern appears to have been derived from the German Aufsteiger. Colour variations are legion, although the version shown is probably the most popular. The pattern can be varied considerably simply by changing the body colour, and I have found a dark-olive version equally successful. The pattern was originally intended to represent the adult sedge with its wings folded tent-like over its body. This insect is particularly at risk during egg-laying, and a variation of the fly includes a bright-yellow butt to represent the egg-cluster. With the buoyant elkhair only lightly greased, so that the body sits in rather than on the water, this pattern is now a firm favourite around the world. It is sometimes tied without the hackle to represent the hatching chironomid or midge pupa.

3   Light Cahill

Hook: Scorpion 31180 all-purpose lightweight, sizes 12–14–16–18–20–22–24.
Tying silk: Very light yellow.
Tail: Cream hackle-fibres.
Body: Creamy seal's fur or substitute, hare's fur or synthetic dubbing.
Wing: Lemon wood-duck or mallard drake grey flank feather dyed lemon.
Hackle: Cream cock.
Head: Clear varnish.

Devised as a winged wet fly, and tied much darker by the Irish-American Dan Cahill, this pattern has evolved to represent the lighter olives in North America. It is also tied in various other guises, such as parachute versions (with the feather wing replaced by calf-body hair) and thorax patterns, as well as the popular nymphs. In its smaller form it is an excellent imitation of caenis (the anglers' curse). This pattern is essential if you fish on limestone or chalk-streams. It should be carried in a variety of sizes, as it is important to match the size of the natural as exactly as possible.

4   Sparklewing Trico

Hook: Orvis 4641 big-eye, sizes 18–20–22–24–26–28.
Tying silk: Black.
Tail: Microfibbets.
Body: Black tying silk.
Wing: Pearlescent Crystal flash.
Thorax: Black synthetic dubbing.
Head: Clear varnish.

It was not until I saw a fall of trico spinners that I believed it possible for trout to become so selective over such a tiny fly. A few years ago, way up in the Rockies, near Denver, I was privileged to witness the astonishing sight of literally billions of spinners forming a mist that was difficult to see through, and fish so preoccupied that you could reach out and touch them on the nose. Of all the patterns we used that day, this Tom Rosenbauer fly, which was still in the experimental stage, proved most effective. Accuracy is essential, and the fly needs to be placed delicately a couple of feet upstream from your quarry and allowed to dead-drift over it. Don't give up if you are ignored several times. The fish have thousands of naturals to choose from, and if the size is right, you will be successful eventually.

5   Weedless Leech

Hook: Long-shank sizes 6–8.
Tying silk: Black.
Underbody: A piece of 20lb breaking-strain nylon tied in to form a hook-point guard.
Overbody: Black floss.
Wing: A strip of black rabbit on skin about ⅛-inch thick and four times the length of the hook-shank.
Head: Black deerhair left shaggy. Clear varnish.
Eyes: Optic eyes (with moving pupils), Superglued on.

This type of fly is used in weedy water for large- and small-mouth bass, the nylon line-guard masking the hook-point and preventing it fouling on pieces of weed. The idea could be incorporated into any type of trout lure. This wiggle-tailed lure has travelled well and catches trout in the UK. Try it also in brown, olive and dark red. The last imitates a worm, making it a good choice in high water.

6   Royal Wulff

Hook: Scorpion 31180 all-purpose lightweight or 31550 all-purpose medium, sizes 8–10–12–14–16–18.
Tying silk: Black.
Tail: Natural elkhair.
Body: Peacock herl with centre band of red rayon floss.
Wing: White calf tail tied upright and divided.
Hackle: Brown cock.
Head: Clear varnish.

No selection of American flies is complete without at least one of Lee Wulff's patterns. 'Wulff' is now a generic term for this style of fly, with divided calf-tail wings, and countless variations are tied. Originally devised as fast-water patterns, these high-floating flies are now used as standards whenever trout are pursued. Following the success of the Royal Coachman, a Wulff version was inevitable and was designed primarily for rainbow trout. However, it has proved highly effective wherever it is fished, and I have taken many good brown trout on smaller sizes. This fly is also an excellent taker of Atlantic salmon, for which it can be tied on single low-water salmon irons up to size 4.

7   Yellow Humpy

Hook: Scorpion 31180 all-purpose lightweight or 31550 all-purpose medium, sizes 8–10–12–14–16–18.
Tying silk: Yellow.
Tail: Natural elkhair.
Body: Yellow rayon floss or tying thread with natural elkhair pulled over to form the back.
Wings: Formed from the tips of the body hair tied upright and divided.
Hackle: Brown and grizzle cock mixed.
Head: Clear varnish.

Another of the classic fast-water patterns from America using elkhair for natural buoyancy, this one is tied in a variety of colours, including a 'Royal' version, but with the red and yellow firm favourites. The Double Humpy is a challenge from a fly-dresser's point of view, particularly in smaller sizes, entailing the tying-in of another set of wings and hackle halfway along the body. The Humpy has undergone various name changes over the years. It was originally known as Horner's Deerhair, and then as the Goofus Bug before it became the Humpy. It is not a specific imitation, but it is extremely effective in fast and broken water. It is worth carrying a full range of sizes to cover all eventualities.

8   Woolly Bugger Black

Hook: Scorpion 32220 traditional streamer, sizes 2–4–6–8–10.
Tying silk: Brown or claret.
Tail: Black marabou.
Underbody: Lead-wire to suit, usually very heavy.
Body: Olive chenille or suede chenille.
Hackle: Black cock, palmered.
Head: Clear varnish.

Anyone restricted to only one streamer-type fly could do far worse than select this popular pattern. And yet in most respects it is not a streamer at all, but a very good imitation of various underwater life-forms, including leeches, stonefly nymphs and dragonfly nymphs. My experience is that this pattern works best on overcast days and often when the water is coloured, when I would generally use the larger sizes. It has accounted for more trout to my rod than I care to remember. On one classic day several years ago on the lower Yellowstone, wading up to my armpits, I took a brownie of 22 inches followed, five minutes later and from the same spot, by a rainbow of 26 inches. Different versions, colours and styles of this fly now abound, including the so-called Nobblers and Leeches, but this one will always be my first choice as a searching pattern and one of the few streamers in my fly-box.

WELSH STILLWATER FLIES

The peaty, acidic stillwaters of Wales are said to be most suited to small brown trout. However, I question this, because I have found good rainbow trout fishing in many lakes and reservoirs all over Wales.

Alun Jenkins, from Neath, has provided six patterns. He tells me they are all proven fish-takers on Welsh reservoirs, but to that I can add that they work well throughout the British Isles and Ireland on lines to suit prevailing conditions.

Mr Griffiths sent me the Bazaar Viva with the comment that 'it leaves all other Viva variations way behind'. He finished by saying, 'Good luck, but you don't need it with this pattern!' The last fly, a fancy pattern from professional tyer Alun Jones, has worked well for me at Grafham, even though it was designed for Llyn Brenig.

---

1   Paul's Choice

Hook: Sproat, sizes 10–12.
Tying silk: Black.
Tail: Glo-Brite floss No. 7, hot-orange.
Body: Orange seal's fur or substitute or Antron.
Rib: Green Crystal hair.
Body hackle: Grizzle cock, palmered.
Hackle: Partridge.
Shoulder hackle: Peacock breast feather.
Head: Blue Flashabou with clear varnish over a normal whip-finish.

This pattern works well from the start of the season through to August, especially when fish are close to the surface. Fish it mainly as a top dropper, but sometimes in the middle. It acts as an attractor to other flies in the team.

---

2   Always

Hook: Sproat sizes 10–12.
Tying silk: Black.
Tail: Black cock hackle-fibres.
Body: Black goose herl.
Rib: Green Crystal hair.
Body hackle: Palmered natural black cock or a dyed substitute.
Wing: Black goose feather-fibre.
Shoulder hackle: Peacock breast feather.
Head: Clear varnish.

Always is another pattern for the large stillwaters, scoring well when the hawthorn or heather-fly begin in early May. Later, it is excellent when the sedges come into season. Try fishing it on a lee shore, where spent adult flies are washed along the wind lanes into the margins, producing a natural larder for the trout.

3 Little Pearl

Hook: Sproat sizes 10–12.
Tying silk: Black.
Tail: Golden pheasant tippet.
Body: Black Antron.
Rib: Glo-Brite floss No. 14, light-blue.
Body hackle: Natural black cock hackle or dyed substitute.
Cheeks: Jungle cock or substitute.
Head: Blue pearl Flashabou with clear varnish over a normal whip-finish.

Alun Jenkins says this is a 'must' on his cast on most fishing days. It is derived from the Black Pennell, but for Alun it works much better and catches fish during all fly-hatches, but especially of chironomids. It can be fished fast on a floater or slow on a sinker, and even as a stationary dry fly.

4 Uplander

Hook: Kamasan B175 sizes 8–10.
Tying silk: Black.
Tag: Red ostrich.
Tail: Golden pheasant crest feather.
Body: Lemon Antron or seal's fur or substitute.
Rib: Fine copper wire.
Body hackle: Yellow and claret cock, half palmered.
Shoulder hackle: Partridge dyed olive.
Head: Clear varnish.

It is difficult to define this pattern's best uses, but mayfly hatches usually determine the time to use it. A static Uplander may be ignored on days when fish become pre-occupied with feeding on adult mayflies, but a fast retrieve and a long 'dabble' of the fly can bring explosive takes. It is also useful as a partner to the Invicta in a traditional team of flies for boat fishing on the big reservoirs.

5 Julie's Pride

Hook: Sproat sizes 10–12.
Tying silk: Black.
Tail: Hen pheasant tail feather-fibres.
Body: Flat gold Lurex.
Rib: Pink wire.
Rear hackle: Hot-orange cock.
Front hackle: White cock.
Head: Clear varnish.

This may appear an unlikely fly, but it has an enviable fish-taking capability in July and August. Gold and orange always have been a good colour combination in these months, as the old Dunkeld proved.

6 Bazaar Viva

Hook: Long-shank sizes 8–10, lead-weighted before dressing.
Tying silk: Black.
Tail: Fluorescent lime-green Lureflash Antron wool.
Body: Lureflash black Frondz.
Wing: Black marabou.
Head: Clear varnish.

Mr Griffiths is adamant that this out and out variation of the popular Viva pattern has an amazing catch-rate. I have not yet tried it, but I shall use it soon, probably on a sinking line.

7 Rebel 15

Hook: Partridge Captain Hamilton, sizes 10–12.
Tying silk: Black.
Tail: Glo-Brite floss No. 15, fluorescent bright purple.
Body: Claret seal's fur or substitute.
Rib: Fine pearl Lurex.
Body hackle: Natural black cock hackle or dyed substitute.
Shoulder hackle: Partridge.
Front hackle: Natural bronze mallard.
Head: Two turns of fine gold Lurex with clear varnish over a normal whip-finish.

The Rebel 15 confirms the value of bright purple and claret in fly-tying. The trout certainly seem to appreciate them. Use this one as top dropper bob-fly in a team of three or four flies from late June through to September. It works best in a big wave, bringing fish to the fly in a 'hypnotic' chase before a slow-motion take.

8 Alun Jones' Fancy

Hook: Kamasan B175 sizes 10–12.
Tying silk: Black.
Tail: Fluorescent-yellow floss and two strands of pearl Flashabou.
Underbody: White floss silk.
Overbody: Pearl Lurex.
Rib: Silver wire.
Body hackle: Yellow cock hackle.
Wings: Four grizzle cock hackle-tips.
Cheeks: Jungle cock or substitute.
Head: Built up, with white Tippex eyes and black varnish pupils.

Alun Jones' fly is a good old-fashioned 'puller': you cast it out as far as you can and then strip back fast. It does best from June to September on floating, sink-tip, intermediate and very slow-sink lines.

FAVOURITE SALMON FLIES

I am certainly no purist when I fish the reservoirs for trout, and at times I use large tandem lures. But for salmon I tend to fish with a fly or tube-fly only. I have caught salmon to more than 20lb on spinner and other big fish on worms, but I was not madly enthusiastic about these methods.

I caught my first salmon, a summer grilse of 7lb, on the Itchen back in 1973.

1 Steve's Red Tube

Hook: A 2-inch copper or brass tube with a size 8 treble hook in a red rubber sleeve.
Tying silk: Black.
Body: Red Bobbydazzlelure.
Rib: Silver Bobbydazzlelure.
Wing: Red bucktail hair, kept long.
Eyes: Large natural jungle cock or substitute.
Head: Clear varnish.

Although my son, Stephen, has never shared the same deep passion for fishing as I have, he is not a bad fly-fisher when he puts his mind to it. He also has binges at the fly-tying bench, usually before our annual back-end trip to the Tweed. This is the most successful of his creations, and as a Tweed fly it has regularly caught big fish for both of us, including seven of 20lb. Red is certainly a good colour for back-end salmon.

2 Mini Tube

Hook: A mini ⅜-inch plastic tube to take a size 12 treble hook.
Tying silk: Black.
Body: Bright-red floss.
Wing: Black squirrel-tail hair.
Head: Black varnish.

A series of these little tubes have brought me some great sport with salmon, and I have the utmost faith in them, especially in summer low water. An experienced Aberdeenshire Dee gillie, Rod Grant, was the first person to stress their value to me. He had used a small black tube to tempt fish when everyone else was failing. I took his advice and soon landed a 7lb summer grilse.

Later, while fishing the Spey tributary, the Avon, I took five June fish to 12lb all on this little black tube with a size 12 treble. The salmon sometimes took it dry in the clear, low-water conditions. Others fishing on the sunny days while I was there used large flies and failed.

Fish it on as light a floating line as you can handle. I hooked more fish when I scaled down my leader to 7lb breaking-strain.

3 Comet

Hook: A 1½-inch brass tube with a size 8 treble hook in a plastic sleeve.
Tying silk: Black.
Tail section: Yellow bucktail.
Body: Rear half, red floss. Now spin on a red bucktail wing. Front half, black floss.
Rib: Gold oval thread.
Wing: Front wing, black bucktail covering full length of tube. Rear wing, as explained in the body section.
Head: Black varnish.

This was the first tube-fly I used with success on the Tweed. In fact, I and many others who fish this river feel it to be the most consistent pattern. Use it on a medium-sink or sink-tip line.

---

4 Stoat's Tail

Hook: Sizes 6–8–10, single, double or treble.
Tying silk: Black.
Tail: Golden pheasant topping.
Body: Black floss silk.
Rib: Silver wire.
Wing: Black squirrel-tail hair.
Throat hackle: Black cock fibres.
Head: Black varnish.

It is often the simplest flies which score best with salmon, and this one just has to be the greatest all-rounder. It will catch salmon—if they are there —whichever river you are on. It is also a great sea-trout, brown trout, rainbow trout and grayling fly.

One successful salmon-fisher I know uses a red tail instead of yellow. It is his favourite fly and he catches a lot of fish on it, year in, year out. Fish it on a floating or sink-tip line in normal or low water.

---

5 Black, Orange and Copper

Hook: a 3-inch copper tube, with a size 6 treble hook in a plastic sleeve.
Tying silk: Black.
Body: Copper Bobbydazzlelure.
Underwing: Orange bucktail, full circle.
Overwing: Black bucktail, full circle.
Head: Black varnish.

A good big visible tube fly which fishes well in heavy coloured water. To be fished on a sinking line and make sure you religiously move that good pace after every case.

6 General Practitioner (modern variant)

Hook: Size 6 or 8 treble or double.
Tying silk: Red.
Tail: Hot-orange bucktail.
Body: Dubbed seal's fur or substitute; mixture of orange with a little pink.
Rib: Fine gold wire.
Body hackle: Palmered long-fibred orange cock.
Underwing: Two full golden pheasant tippet hackle-feathers.
Overwing: One or two long-fibred soft golden pheasant red breast feathers.
Head: Clear varnish.

Esmond Drury was a brilliant military man and this made him an excellent tactitian on the river. When he was faced with some difficult salmon on the Test, he decided a fly which looked rather like a shrimp or prawn, but was made from fur and feather, should work well. He devised the GP, and simply to say that it did well is an understatement. It has won fame wherever Atlantic salmon are fished for. It can be fished on all types of line according to river conditions, but the heavier the water, the larger the fly should be. This pattern is a variant of Esmond Drury's original.

---

7 Dr Gardner's Tube

Hook: A 1¾-inch copper tube with a size 8 treble hook in a plastic sleeve.
Tying silk: Black.
Wing: Yellow and black bucktail, evenly mixed.
Head: Black varnish.

For several years I stayed at the Ednam House Hotel, Kelso, for a week's back-end fishing on the Tweed. Dr John Gardner was always there for the same week, when we all hoped to catch a few grey-backs. John always caught his fair share, and this was his favourite fly. An orange-and-black variant was also used, again over a plain copper body.

---

8 Twilight Fly

Hook: A 2-inch copper tube with a size 8 treble hook in a plastic sleeve.
Tying silk: Black.
Body: Silver Mylar tubing.
Rib: Fuse wire.
Wing: White bucktail, full circle.
Head: Black varnish.

It was my good fishing friend Brian Furzer who introduced me to this white tube-fly. He had found that it worked well as the evening light began to fade, hence its name. Brian has landed salmon to 23lb on this fly, but they have always been hooked at twilight—room for thought here.

SEA-TROUT SPECIALS

Sadly, that great sporting fish, the sea-trout, has been declining in numbers in parts of the UK and Ireland. Since the mid-eighties we have seen some of the best sea-trout fly-fishing in the west of Ireland fall to nothing, due in part, we are told, to the cage-rearing of fish in the sea. It is a long and complicated story, but I did see signs of a recovery in 1990 on the Costello Fishery in County Mayo. Mike Childs and I caught 24 fish to 2½lb in three drifts, all returned. Let's hope for a return to normal soon.

Plenty of good sea-trout fishing is still to be had. All the east-coast rivers of northern England and Scotland stayed good, and the fishing in Scandinavia is better than ever, with Sweden's famous Morrum excelling. During a visit in September 1992 I heard of eight sea-trout of more than 20lb caught in just four days.

---

1 All Suck (Morrum Shrimp)

Hook: Sizes 4–6; single salmon hook.
Tying silk: Black.
Tail: Scarlet hackle-fibres with a few fibres from a golden pheasant rump feather.
Body: Black floss.
Rear wing: A mixture of orange and pearl Crystal tied sparse.
Body hackle: Medium ginger cock.
Head hackle: Medium ginger cock.
Head: Black varnish.

My Morrum fishing guide, Issac, used this fly all the time in one form or another. It seems to work well for both the big sea-trout and the salmon from this impressive river. It can be tied on doubles, trebles or tubes, but a single-hook rule was in force when I was there following a dry summer and low water. The single hook helps to avoid accidental foul-hooking.

Fish this fly on a floating sink-tip or sinking lines according to conditions. I found it possible to fish a size 2 single on a 3-inch tube-fly, though whether the hooking ratio is as good with a single as with a treble is debatable. Try this fly on any water where sea-trout run.

---

2 Conway Red

Hook: Sizes 6–8; single salmon hook.
Tying silk: Black.
Body: Black floss silk.
Rib: Red Lurex tinsel.
Hackle: Ginger hen.
Wing: Grey squirrel-tail hair.
Head: Clear or black varnish.

This fly from North Wales was originally tied with a badger hair wing, *i.e.* similarly to Cyril Inwood's old fly. However, substituting grey squirrel-tail hair has made no difference to its fish-catching ability. It travels well. Try it on Scottish sea-trout rivers and you will see what I mean.

3 The Great Western

Hook: Sizes 8–10.
Tying silk: Black.
Tail: A thick bunch of yellow cock hackle-fibres, or golden pheasant crest.
Body: Black Antron, kept slim.
Rib: Fine silver oval thread.
Hackle: Rear one-third, black; centre one-third, bright red; front one-third, black; palmered.
Head: Black varnish.

This is a great fly for the West of Ireland loughs. I have caught sea-trout with it on Beltra, Innagh, Costello, Feeagh and Furnace. Nothing is more pleasurable than to drift along with a good fishing pal and gillie catching sea-trout off the top. With a steady wind, this is a fly to bring fish up to the top dropper. Another good fly to have on the cast is a Daddy-long-legs (*see* trout section).

---

4 Tywi Special

Hook: Size 8 treble, attached to 1½-inch Waddington shank.
Tying silk: Red.
Tail: Just whip the treble hook-shank red.
Body: Pearl Mylar tubing over shank.
Hackle: Very long-fibred saddle, dyed bright-red.
Wing: A few strands of pearl Crystal and two strands of bronze peacock herl.
Head: Red varnish; also red-varnished tail.

This fly was given to me by Dr Graeme Harris, a Tywi (or Towy) expert. Graeme has fished the river for many years, taking hundreds of sea-trout. He described this pattern as '... a bit special ... Catches most of my fish on the Tywi ...' Need I say more? It is primarily a fly for night fishing, and it is only when you experience the thrill of a big hooked sea-trout after dark as you wade in the middle of a river that you truly know what fly-fishing is all about.

---

5 Cyril Inwood's Conway Fly

Hook: Size 8. Make up a three-hook rig as shown by connecting with 20lb breaking-strain nylon and whipping tight.
Tying silk: White.
Bodies: Silver tinsel (now tarnished; *see* below).
Throat hackle: Blue cock hackle-fibres.
Wing: Badger hair.
Eyes: Jungle cock or substitute.
Head: Clear varnish.

I did say that I wouldn't include any old flies, but you will realize why I couldn't resist this one. Cyril Inwood was a brilliant fisherman. He took me under his wing not long before he died in 1971 and passed on quite a few good tips. Cyril and his friend, Frank Cutler, were masters at fishing the big sea-trout of the Conway in North Wales. They always took the last two weeks in July, when they stayed at Betws-y-Coed. They fished a famous sea-trout pool called Havard's, and it was here they caught many massive fish. Cyril's best was 18½lb to this very fly, which he gave me as a souvenir. He said it was the best night sea-trout fly for big fish he had ever tried. Forgive this tarnished and battered original Cyril Inwood fly. He would have been so pleased that I told you this tale. Nice one, Cyril!

6 All-rounder

Hook: Sizes 6–8; single salmon hook.
Tying silk: Black.
Tail: Golden pheasant topping.
Body: Black seal's fur or substitute.
Rib: Wide silver oval thread.
Hackle: Black cock.
Wing: Black squirrel hair overlaid with red squirrel and then four peacock sword feathers.
Eyes: Jungle cock or substitute as here.
Head: Clear or black varnish.

The All-rounder is known to produce good catches of sea-trout when used as a wake fly. This means allowing the current to sweep the fly round in fast water, or, in slower-flowing water, giving the fly speed by stripping it back fast.

7 Dovey Black and Orange

Hook: Sizes 6–8; single salmon hook.
Tying silk: Black.
Tail: Swan feather dyed red.
Body: Black floss silk.
Rib: Medium silver oval thread.
Hackle: Orange hen.
Wing: Black squirrel-tail hair.
Eyes: Jungle cock or substitute.
Head: Clear or black varnish.

Said to fish as well by day as it does at night, this is a star performer in high water. If you use it at night, fish it with a good sinking line and retrieve the fly along the bottom. It has accounted for many big fish from its home river.

8 Blue Knight

Hook: Sizes 6–8, with a size 12 or 14 flying treble attached as a tandem.
Tying silk: Black.
Tail: Fluorescent-pink floss or treble shank.
Body: Silver tinsel.
Rib: Gold oval thread.
Throat hackle: Orange cock fibres.
Wing: Four blue cock hackles, flanked by two hen grizzle hackles and topped by three long peacock sword strands.
Head: Clear or black varnish.

Another favourite of regulars on the famous Welsh sea-trout rivers, this pattern is known as a big-fish attractor at night. Blue often appears in the better Welsh sea-trout flies.

Top of the Water Flies

CUL-DE-CANARD DRY FLIES

The biggest talking point in 1992 was the *cul-de-canard* series of dry flies based on the little *cul-de-canard* feathers which come from a duck's tail area and are impregnated by its oil gland. The birds often carry as few as ten such feathers, and at most thirty. Being naturally well-oiled, these feathers are water-repellent and, tied into a fly as hackle or a wing, produce a dry fly that needs no greasing. Supplies are limited.

---

1 Cul-de-canard Black Gnat

Hook: Sizes 14–16, light wire.
Tying silk: Black.
Body: Black micro-chenille (also known as Easy Dub).
Hackle: Natural *cul-de-canard* feather.
Head: Clear varnish.

So many different species of small black fly hatch from the water or are blown on to it that it pays to have a good representative pattern. This *Cul-de-canard* Black Gnat dry fly is just right for the job. It has scored best on rivers, where it is very visible even at long range under over-hanging far-bank trees.

---

2 Cul-de-canard Blue Dun

Hook: Sizes 14–16, light wire.
Tying silk: Brown.
Body: Dark-grey micro-chenille.
Hackle: Natural *cul-de-canard* feather.
Head: Clear varnish.

Many river fly-fishers say that the Blue Dun is the deadliest of all their flies, beating even the olives and blacks, so they were bound to show interest in an uncomplicated, nonsinkable version. This fly has quickly become popular with all chalkstream and rain-fed river fishers.

3 Cul-de-canard Light Olive

Hook: Sizes 12–14, light wire.
Tying silk: Orange.
Body: Dyed light-olive turkey or goose feather-fibre.
Wing: Natural *cul-de-canard* feather-fibres.
Head: Clear varnish.

This style of tying is for use during calm conditions on stillwaters. The hook and body of the fly sink into the surface film, while the floating wing keeps it in that important position. Ascending chironomids emerge in this manner, and we all now know that trout take a fly best at the moment of emergence. Fished in the right place, this pattern does best when used on its own.

4 Cul-de-canard Dark Olive

Hook: Sizes 12–14, light wire.
Tying silk: Orange.
Body: Dark-olive polypropylene.
Rib: Thin pearl Lurex.
Wing: Natural *cul-de-canard* feather-fibres.
Head: Clear varnish.

A more robust tying of an olive dry fly, this one serves during both olive and chironomid hatches. It fishes nicely in a light ripple, when the best floating action is achieved by all the winged versions of these flies. The amazing thing about all these cul-de-canard dry flies is that if you pull the leader, causing the fly to sink, it pops up, floating high on the surface again, as soon as you pause.

5 Cul-de-canard Claret

Hook: Sizes 12–14, light wire.
Tying silk: Orange.
Body: Claret micro-chenille.
Wing: Natural *cul-de-canard* feather-fibre.
Head: Clear varnish.

Claret was prominent in a number of dry-fly patterns in 1992, and many of them were extremely successful, with reservoir trout seeming to pick out this colour in preference to others. It was natural that a *cul-de-canard* version soon outfished other styles.

6   Cul-de-canard Orange

Hook: Sizes 12–14, light wire.
Tying silk: Orange.
Body: Orange micro-chenille.
Wing: Natural *cul-de-canard* feather-fibre.
Head: Clear varnish.

Although various body materials can be used in conjunction with *cul-de-canard* featherwings, Veniard's Easy Dub micro-chenille takes some beating for tying a quick fly. It is very light, comes in a range of colours, and forms a slim, even, yet hairy, body.

I use this orange *cul-de-canard* fly when big ginger buzzers are coming off major reservoirs. I took four fish of more than 2lb in a flat-calm heatwave while trial fishing this pattern at Chew Valley. It later worked well on all the Midlands reservoirs.

7   Cul-de-canard Rusty

Hook: Sizes 12–14, light wire.
Tying silk: Black.
Body: Dubbed rusty-brownish-orange polypropylene, tied twice as thick as in the other patterns.
Rib: Pearl or gold Lurex.
Wing: A generous portion of natural *cul-de-canard* feather-fibre.
Head: Black varnish.

This fly is deliberately tied in generous proportions so as to be easily fished in rough water, floating high and remaining visible. If you are fishing from a drifting boat and wind lanes cross the reservoir, position the boat to enable you to cast this fly into one of them. Fish it static or with slow figure-of-eight retrieve.

8   Cul-de-canard Yellow

Hook: Sizes 12–14, light wire.
Tying silk: Orange.
Body: Yellow Antron or any modern seal's fur substitute.
Wing: Natural *cul-de-canard* feather-fibre.
Head: Clear varnish.

This is a good fly to use when sedges are about in mid-summer. Concentrate on evening fishing in quiet shallow bays on the upwind shore. Fish it by itself in a flat calm on a 3lb breaking-strain degreased leader point. Static is best unless lots of skating, egg-laying sedges are on the water, when a retrieve can work well.

MAGICAL MAYFLIES: DRY FLIES

Even as we approach the end of the twentieth century, fly-fishermen wait for mayfly time just as eagerly as their forebears did a hundred years ago. Some English rivers may not be as good as they were, but probably more mayfly are about now than ever before. This is due mainly to the creation of lovely, landscaped gravel-pit fisheries all over the Midlands, the Cotswolds and the South of England. Massive hatches of mayfly occur on these rich waters, and magical sport can be had for two or three weeks each season.

Mayfly time was long ago christened 'duffer's fortnight'. Nothing has changed—except for the tackle with which we catch our fish and the range of fly-tying materials. With both we are much better off than our forefathers.

---

1 Olive Mask Mayfly

Hook: Size 8.
Tying silk: Black.
Tail: Pheasant tail feather-fibres.
Body: Cream silk.
Rib: Red thread.
Hackle: Long-fibred light-ginger/honey cock.
Wing: A pair of mallard breast feathers dyed olive and tied fanwing-style.
Head: Clear varnish.

This fanwing olive is of the type so favoured on the big west-of-Ireland loughs. It may not be new, but I rate it highly simply because of its consistency. Use it with every confidence during late May and early June on Mask, Corrib, Carra and Conn.

---

2 Yellow Mask Mayfly

Hook: Size 8.
Tying silk: Black.
Tail: Pheasant tail feather-fibres.
Body: Yellow floss silk.
Rib: Fine gold oval thread.
Hackle: Long-fibred medium-brown cock.
Wing: A pair of lemon wood-duck or mallard breast feathers dyed yellow and tied fanwing-style.
Head: Clear varnish.

I found this fly for the Irish limestone loughs in Art O'Neil's bar in the little town of Ballinrobe, County Mayo, a stone's throw from Lough Mask and Cushlough Bay. Gillies such as Robbie O'Grady, Jimmy Murphy, Noel May and Michael Harness have taken me out from there, and each has recommended this mayfly. Ah! Sweet memories!

3 Detached Fanwing Mayfly

Hook: Sizes 8–10, up-eyed.
Tying silk: Black.
Detached tail and body: Thread three strands of cock pheasant tail feather-fibres through your bought detached hollow latex body and tie this in on top of the hook-shank and well behind the eye.
Wing: A pair of lemon wood-duck breast feathers or silver mallard dyed yellow.
Hackle: Long fibres of badger cock.
Head: Clear varnish.

The inclusion of the moulded latex detached body gives this pattern a lifelike silhouette. Detached bodies are not new, but this very soft one, with its segmented rib, is the best yet. It's worth buying a few of these bodies and experimenting with them at the tying bench. Fish this pattern alone and static when mayfly are hatching.

4 Rafael's Yellow Mayfly (spent)

Hook: Size 10.
Tying silk: Brown Gossamer.
Tail: Natural cock-of-Leon feather-fibres (similar to grizzle).
Body: Brown tying silk butt, leading on to a fine, yellow silk body.
Rib: Brown tying silk.
Wings: Two pairs of cock-of-Leon hackle-tips dyed yellow and tied spent.
Hackle: Finely half-palmered cock of Leon dyed yellow.
Head: Clear varnish.

Over the last ten years I have had a number of very special flies given to me by my good Spanish friend, Rafael de Madriago, from Madrid. Rafael's fly-fishing partner is Rafael del Pozo, and it is he who creates these magnificent patterns. He is Spain's leading authority on fly-tying.

The cock of Leon is an especially prized bird which produces superb hackles marked similarly to those from a top-quality grizzle cape. These are dyed in various shades and, being so stiff-fibred, are used to make really high-floating dry flies. I have used this spent pattern with great success on a variety of waters.

5 Rafael's Grizzle Mayfly (spent)

Hook: Size 10.
Tying silk: Brown Gossamer.
Tail: Natural cock-of-Leon feather-fibres.
Body: Brown tying silk butt leading on to a fine, off-white silk body.
Wings: Two pairs of natural cock-of-Leon hackle-tips tied spent.
Hackle: Finely half-palmered natural cock of Leon.
Head: Clear varnish.

This natural cock-of-Leon hackle version is again a spent pattern which is, of course, at its best in the evening. All these dry flies from Spain have worked equally well on river, lake and lough.

6 Detached Emerging Mayfly

Hook: Sizes 8–10, up-eyed.
Tying silk: Black.
Detached tail and body: Thread three strands of cock pheasant tail feather-fibres through the hollow latex detached body. Tie this in on the top of the hook shank well behind the eye.
Hackle: Long-fibred light-blue dun hen at rear; speckled French partridge hackle at front.
Head: Clear varnish.

Lots of mayfly hatch when a warm westerly wind is giving a good wave, especially on the Irish lough. The hatch often begins in semi-sheltered areas, such as around rocky islands. Soon, though, the flies are blown off by the wind, sometimes falling on the surface. A good tactic in these conditions is to try a hackled emerging or struggling mayfly artificial, and this one suits the situation well. Use it as a top dropper and skim it back through the waves before bobbing it for a few seconds.

7 Rafael's Hackled Mayfly

Hook: Size 10.
Tying silk: Black.
Tail: Long strands of fine, black hair.
Body: Brownish/yellow silk.
Rib: Black tying silk.
Hackle: Natural cock of Leon at rear; cock of Leon dyed brownish/yellow at front.
Head: Clear varnish.

This is a robust, general-purpose dry mayfly. These four Spanish designs are by far the best I have ever come across, and I heartily endorse them. If you cannot obtain the expensive and rare cock-of-Leon hackles, substitute a top-quality grizzle cock cape and dye it the shades you need.

8 Rafael's Dark-olive Mayfly

Hook: Size 10.
Tying silk: Black.
Tail: Six strands of long, fine black hair.
Body: Dull-yellow silk, carrot-shaped.
Rib: Black tying silk.
Wing: A pair of cock-of-Leon hackles dyed dark-olive and tied upright.
Hackle: A top-rate selected cock dyed dark-olive.
Head: Clear varnish.

Flies of this deadly pattern look so realistic that trout, rainbows or browns, seem to be easily fooled into thinking they are the real thing. Once on a Cotswolds fishery I had to take this fly off. It really was that good!

MAGICAL MAYFLIES: DRY, WET AND NYMPH

These two sets of dry and dry/wet mayflies include one or two older patterns that work as well in the nineties as they ever have.

---

1 Charles's Little Mayfly

Hook: Size 12.
Tying silk: Black.
Tail: Golden pheasant tippets.
Body: Yellow floss.
Rib: Black tying silk.
Wing: A bunch of lemon wood-duck feather-fibres tied upright and forward.
Hackle: Light ginger cock.
Head: Clear varnish.

Use this when trout are in a funny mood, rising to the artificial but only splashing at it. This smaller pattern was given to me by Charles Jardine to try on such occasions, and it works well during the tail-end of mayfly time, mid-June, when only a few naturals remain.

---

2 Church-Little Mayfly

Hook: Sizes 12–14.
Tying silk: Black.
Tail: Brownish/olive cock hackle-fibres.
Body: Light-brown tying silk.
Rib: Cream tying silk.
Wing: Either a pair of golden pheasant topping feathers or a few fibres of lemon wood-duck tied upright.
Hackle: Brownish/olive cock.
Head: Clear varnish.

Use for exactly the same reasons as the previous little dry mayfly. This has worked for me on rivers, the Irish limestone loughs and at small fisheries like Church Hill Farm, Lechlade in the Cotswolds and Bishops Bowl.

3 Cyril Inwood's Original Mayfly

Hook: Sizes 8–10.
Tying silk: Black.
Tail: Pheasant tail feather-fibres.
Butt: Brown tying silk varnished.
Body: A strip of cork.
Rib: Brown tying silk.
Wing: Artificial wing lace cut to shape.
Hackle: Light coch-y-bondhu.
Head: Clear varnish.

This pattern was given to me by veteran Frank Cutler, who was given it by Cyril Inwood, who died in 1971. Cyril was one of the all-time greats at all branches of freshwater fishing. This dry mayfly looks really natural in its drab colours, and it must be one of Cyril's own tyings.

4 Orange-Hackled Mayfly

Hook: Sizes 8–10.
Tying silk: Black.
Tail: Pheasant tail feather-fibres.
Body: Light-olive Antron.
Body hackle: Greenwell's cock.
Rear hackle: Long-fibred hot-orange cock.
Front hackle: Grey partridge.
Head: Clear varnish.

This Mayfly can be fished dry or wet-dry, just subsurface, as conditions dictate, and is another great pattern for wet and windy days when you are boat fishing on a water with a mayfly hatch. Use it as a top dropper, as I have with success on lovely Lough Conn out from Pontoon Bridge. The tactic is to retrieve a team of three through the waves and then bob this fly for several seconds on the surface before re-casting.

5 Brian Thomas Wet Mayfly

Hook: Sizes 8–10.
Tying silk: Primrose.
Body: Golden-olive seal's fur or substitute or Antron.
Rib: Fine gold or silver wire.
Wing: A slip of natural bronze mallard.
Hackle: Golden pheasant tippet feather.
Head: Clear varnish.

Brian tied me half-a-dozen of these flies when we fished an International at Lough Conn. The pattern had won the Brown Bowl (individual winner) two years earlier on the same water for English team member Derek Stenner, when he caught eight good trout in Cloghan's Bay.

The fly has produced its best results when used with a slow-sinking line. It seems likely that the trout take it for the ascending mayfly nymph.

124

6 Fluorescent Mayfly

Hook: Sizes 8–10, painted matt green.
Tying silk: Black.
Tail: Pheasant tail feather-fibres.
Body: Fluorescent-yellow chenille.
Wing: A bunch of deerhair dyed yellow.
Hackle: Bright-yellow long-fibred cock.
Head: Clear varnish.

I devised this pattern to be used in a really high wave on Irish loughs, when cruder, high-visibility flies can be more easily seen by trout which feed confidently in these awkward fishing conditions. The fly is best retrieved quite quickly, as you would a Muddler Minnow. Trout then strike the fly without having much time to inspect it. It worked for me on Mask and Carra.

7 Yellow Mayfly Nymph

Hook: Long-shank only, sizes 8–10.
Tying silk: Black or brown.
Tail: Yellow cock hackle-fibres.
Body: Yellow seal's fur or substitute.
Rib: Fine silver wire or oval thread.
Hackle: Medium-brown hen.
Shellback: Brown feather-fibre.
Head: Clear varnish.

This one is for use on any stillwater, ideally when fish are not rising at all before the mayfly season starts. The quite large nymphs are often active in the bottom silt before they hatch, and this nymph, fished on an intermediate or slow-sinking line, simulates this movement. Use a slow figure-of-eight retrieve.

8 Gilled Mayfly Nymph

Hook: Long-shank size 10; leaded underbody optional.
Tying silk: Brown.
Tail: Cock pheasant tail fibres.
Tag: Brown Antron.
Body: Pale hare's fur.
Rib: Buff ostrich herl.
Over-rib: Brown tying silk.
Thorax: Pale cream hare's fur.
Wing-cases: Cock pheasant tail fibres.
Legs: Cock pheasant tail fibres.
Head: Clear varnish.

This life-like Mayfly Nymph is ideal for use in stillwater or river. It can be used at any time of the season, but is best from early May until the end of June. The ostrich herl perfectly imitates this large nymph's gills. Another Peter Gathercole pattern with a good success rate.

125

HOPPERS AND DADDIES

For British fly-fishers, Hoppers started life at Grafham Water in the late nineteen-eighties. I remember fishing with Andy Linwood in a boat during an August heatwave. The water was flat, but Andy put on a Claret Hopper and caught a couple of nice rainbows before lunch, while I was blank. That was the first time I had seen this fly, and at the time it was still on the secret list of the successful Grafham Fly Fishers team.

The Pioneers of this now widely accepted dry-fly style, apart from Andy, were Bob Worts, Dave Barker and John Moore. Once the method had leaked out, it was soon adopted by top fly-fishers at Bristol, for it was well suited to Chew Valley Lake.

A whole series of Hoppers is now available. Also included are new 'Daddies'.

---

1 Black Hopper

Hook: Sizes 10–12.
Tying silk: Black.
Body: Black Antron dubbed on.
Rib: Fine pearl Lurex.
Legs: Six pairs of cock pheasant tail fibres, knotted once and tied in at the head, three each side, so that they trail back.
Hackle: Three turns of black cock.
Head: Clear varnish.

So many black flies end up on the surface of trout lakes that the fish become used to rising and taking them, whether they be hawthorn flies, black gnats, heather-flies or black chironomids. The Black Hopper is accepted by the trout with such confidence that to them it must appear as just another tasty morsel. All the Hoppers in this series should be lightly treated with Gink flotant to ensure they never sink, even in a high wave.

---

2 Brown Hopper

Hook: Sizes 10–12.
Tying silk: Black.
Body: Brown Antron dubbed on.
Rib: Fine pearl Lurex.
Legs: Six pairs tied in at the head (as in the Black Hopper).
Hackle: Three turns of brown cock.
Head: Clear varnish.

The Brown Hopper is most like a mini-Daddy-long-legs. It has been very successful for me, especially at Rutland. While fishing the shallows of the South Arm in early July 1991, I took limits of quality fish on three occasions when others were finding the going difficult.

I also hit the jackpot at Bayham Lake, in Kent, with this same fly after all else had failed. This time it was on a quite cold day in October. No fish were rising, but I thought I would try a size 12 Brown Hopper. The result was a splashy rise and a four-pounder on the bank. The fish came up from nowhere in an area which had been heavily fished in conventional style for half the day. I finished with eight trout caught in thirty minutes, all on the same fly.

3 Yellow Hopper

Hook: Sizes 10–12.
Tying silk: Black.
Body: Yellow Antron dubbed on.
Rib: Fine pearl Lurex; alternative, gold.
Legs: Six pairs tied in at the head as in the Black Hopper.
Hackle: Three turns of light-ginger cock.
Head: Clear varnish.

It was the well-known 'Geordie' Chris Guthrie who stressed the worth of this pattern. Chris had been a top-class professional footballer until the age of thirty-two and had then put all his sporting effort into his second love, fly-fishing for trout and salmon.

Practising at Grafham for a big competition, he suddenly found success in a big way with the Yellow Hopper. Sometimes a small yellow crane-fly gets on to the water in summer, but only in small numbers. I am not sure whether the two are connected, but I do know that what Chris found out still works well at Grafham and elsewhere during high summer. Remember to fish this one static.

4 Olive Hopper

Hook: Sizes 10–12.
Tying silk: Black or olive.
Body: Medium-olive Antron dubbed on.
Rib: Fine pearl Lurex.
Legs: Six pairs tied in at the head as in the Black Hopper.
Hackle: Three turns of medium-olive cock.
Head: Clear varnish.

This is a good general pattern similar to the black one. Many olives are on the water in late May and again in September, but olive chironomids appear from April through to autumn. You have to be an opportunist and try this one when you feel conditions are right.

5 Dark Daddy-long-legs (Cranefly)

Hook: Sizes 8–10.
Tying silk: Black or brown.
Body: Tied as a detached, dark-coloured, thick deerhair tube, secured at head.
Legs: Six pairs, trailing.
Wing: A pair of wide Greenwell's cock.
Hackle: Two dark-ginger cock.
Head: Clear varnish.

This version is used in similar style to the Light Daddy, and, being more 'meaty' looking, works well on a dapping rod and blowline. This is a favourite and deadly method on the Irish loughs.

6 Claret Hopper

Hook: Sizes 10–12.
Tying silk: Black.
Body: Dark claret Antron dubbed on.
Rib: Fine pearl Lurex.
Legs: Six pairs tied in at the head as in the Black Hopper.
Hackle: Three turns of red or claret cock.
Head: Clear varnish.

Claret was the colour to use in a floating fly during 1992. Trout at Grafham, Rutland, Pitsford, Draycote and Chew Valley all seemed to be picking out this colour.

7 Light Daddy-long-legs (Cranefly)

Hook: Sizes 8–10.
Tying silk: Primrose.
Body: Tied as a detached light-coloured deerhair tube secured at head.
Legs: Two pairs of long trailing legs, one pair shorter, tied vertically at the hook-eye.
Wing: A pair of cree cock hackle-tips tied spent.
Hackle: One light-ginger and one honey cock, mixed.
Head: Clear varnish.

Fish this one singly on a long leader and floating line. A stationary fly or one being fished only by the breeze is usually best, but on some days a steady retrieve against the breeze produces quite violent takes. Slightly heavier nylon is then needed to avoid breakages.

8 Orange Hopper

Hook: Sizes 10–12.
Tying silk: Black or brown.
Body: Rusty-orange Antron mix dubbed on.
Rib: Fine pearl Lurex.
Legs: Six pairs tied in at head (as in the Black Hopper).
Hackle: Three turns of red or dark claret cock.
Head: Clear varnish.

This is similar to the pattern I saw Andy Linwood using on Grafham, but another version has a much fatter body. Many experts fish two or three at once, at least two metres apart. Fish this one static.

STILLWATER DRY FLIES

It was in the late nineteen-eighties that a group of dedicated Grafham fly-fishers began to have some marvellous results with new dry-fly patterns at this big water. Before this, apart from during the daddy-long-legs, drone-fly, and occasional sedge-fly times, dry fly was looked upon as an inferior method.

The men responsible for the now incredible popularity of the method were Bob Worts (who pioneered the first dry emerging chironomids—Bob's Bits), Andy Linwood, John Moore and Dave Barker (who were more into the original Claret Hopper), and Dave Shipman (with his simple floating emerging chironomids). Known as Shipman's Buzzers, these have become national favourites, working on all reservoirs and, I hear, on lochs as well.

---

1 Rusty-orange Shipman's Buzzer

Hook: Sizes 10–12
Tying silk: Orange.
Tail: White wool.
Body: Rusty-orange seal's fur or substitute.
Rib: Pearl Lurex.
Breather: White wool.
Head: Clear varnish.

One of the early successes from Dave's series of dry buzzer emergers was this rusty-orange version. Many hatches of large buzzers at the major reservoirs have this coloration, and this is my favourite. Fish one, two or even three, well spaced out and smeared in Gink to ensure high floating. It is important that the nylon leader and droppers are degreased to ensure they sink a little, leaving just the flies on the surface for the trout to see. Takes will be confident if this practice is followed, with fewer spooked fish shying away from the floating nylon.

---

2 Black Shipman's Buzzer

Hook: Sizes 10–12.
Tying silk: Black.
Tail: White wool.
Body: Black seal's fur or substitute.
Rib: Pearl Lurex.
Breather: White wool.
Head: Clear or black varnish.

Black is always a popular and successful base colour for submerged buzzer patterns, so it is hardly surprising that a black version of Dave's emerger catches a lot of fish. It is very good on dark, windy days, when trout seem to pick it out well.

3 Red Shipman's Buzzer

Hook: Sizes 10–12.
Tying silk: Black or red.
Tail: White wool.
Body: Red seal's fur or substitute.
Rib: Pearl Lurex.
Breather: White wool.
Head: Clear varnish.

Red has been used with success in surface flies, especially emergers, only in recent years. Fish will at times nose this fly before taking confidently and leisurely swimming off. Takes can therefore be very slow, and you need to watch your floating fly carefully. It is fair to assume that fish often hook themselves when this happens, but a timely strike ensures success.

4 Olive Shipman's Buzzer

Hook: Sizes 10–12.
Tying silk: Black or yellow.
Tail: White wool.
Body: Light-olive seal's fur or substitute.
Rib: Pearl Lurex.
Breather: White wool.
Head: Clear varnish.

During late May and June, not only do we have the upwinged olives on the water, but also good hatches of olive buzzers. Some of these are large, such as the big orange/ginger buzzers, and need to be imitated in size with the use of a size 10 hook. This pattern does well when these nymphs are emerging.

With all these Shipman's emergers, and with any others, keep your leader as fine as possible in light breezes or calm conditions. However, in a good wave a 6lb breaking-strain leader can be used with confidence and equal chances of a take. With the stronger nylon, if you do hit a big fish, you are sure of netting it.

5 Olive Bob's Bits

Hook: Size 12.
Tying silk: Black.
Tail: Ginger cock hackle-fibres.
Body: Olive Antron.
Rib: Fine silver oval thread.
Wing: White duck feather-fibre.
Hackle: Ginger cock.
Head: Clear varnish.

This pattern is deliberately tied with more dressing than the others in this set because it does well in a wave. It has been by far my most successful Bob's Bits pattern at Grafham, Rutland, Pitsford and Draycote. If the fish are finnicky, fish this pattern singly and watch results improve.

6 Brown Bob's Bits

Hook: Sizes 10–12.
Tying silk: Black or brown.
Body: Three-quarters hare's ear fur-fibres dyed brown; one-quarter orange Antron. Keep the body carrot-shaped.
Rib: Tying silk.
Wing: A few white feather-fibres halfway up the shank.
Hackle: Medium-brown cock.
Head: Clear varnish.

It was on this pattern, more similar to Bob Wort's original design, introduced on Grafham, that Bob landed the first-ever 10lb-plus rainbow from this famous reservoir. Bob is left-handed and makes his cast not straight downwind, but more to the side of the boat's drifting path. He makes a shortish (maximum 10 metres) cast, takes up the slack as the boat drifts on, and continuously repeats the process. The flies are always static.

7 Orange Bob's Bits

Hook: Size 12.
Tying silk: Brown or orange.
Tag: Pearl Lurex right round bend.
Body: Tying silk.
Wing: White feather-fibre.
Hackle: Dark ginger fibres on top of hook only.
Head: Clear varnish.

Whether the pearl tag gives this version the edge is a matter for you to decide. On its day it can be deadly and the pick of the cast.

8 Red Bob's Bits

Hook: Sizes 12–14.
Tying silk: White.
Body: Bright red seal's fur or Antron.
Rib: Tying silk.
Wing: Three or four white feather-fibres.
Head: Clear varnish.

This is one for Rutland or Grafham in high summer, July or August. It doesn't matter if it's been hot, it doesn't matter if it's a flat calm, rainbows cruising just beneath the surface will come up and take it. You need to see it happen to believe it, so try this simple little blob of red fished on a fine leader. Use as light a floating line as you can for all these stillwater dries which usually means lines rated AFTM 5, 6 and 7.

133

PALMERS

Nobody who fishes the reservoirs, Scottish lochs or Irish loughs can afford to be without a good range of palmer-hackled flies. They are used mostly as top droppers, causing a disturbance as they are fished back through the wave tops towards the drifting boat.

The method known as loch-style drifting with a team of three or four wet flies has gained in popularity during the last few years. Fly-fishers love to fish in this way because it causes so much excitement for two sharing a boat. It is normal to have more offers by way of fish merely boiling at the fly, or sometimes splashing at it as they try to drown it. I often grease a palmered fly to ensure that it floats even in the biggest wave.

---

1 Hot-spot Wickham's

Hook: Sizes 10–12–14.
Tying silk: Use the colour chosen for the 'hot-spot', in this case orange.
Tail: Fluorescent-orange Glo-Brite multi-yarn.
Body: Gold Lurex.
Rib: Fine gold oval thread.
Hackle: Ginger cock, palmered.
Thorax: Fluorescent-orange seal's fur or substitute.
Head: Clear varnish.

It was at Rutland that these flies had their first success. Terry Oliver had practised for the Midlands final and caught six fish on a lime-green Hot-spot Wickham's. He gave me one on match-day morning and I caught a couple of bonus fish on it during the slow midday period. The seven fish I caught that day gave me a place in the following year's England team. But I would not have been selected with only five fish!

I have since developed the fly into a series, and it is this orange version which works best for me in high summer and autumn. Use it as a point-fly in a good wave, as well as in the more traditional top dropper position, and stay with a floating line. Other colours to try, all fluorescent, are lime-green, red, yellow and pink. Of natural colours, olive, brown, grey and black are all worth consideration.

---

2 Eilden's Pink Palmer

Hook: Sizes 10–12–14.
Tying silk: Black.
Body: Gold Lurex.
Rib: Fine gold oval thread.
Hackle: Washed-out pink cock hackle, palmered.
Head: Clear varnish.

John Eilden, from Bedford, has been a prominent boat fly-fisherman on the Midlands reservoirs for many years, but he is not the sort of person who regularly invents new flies. In fact, this is the only one I know which bears his name.

John put in several good competition performances with this pattern, with wins at Grafham and Rutland. Its secret, he claimed, was the all-important washed-out pink body hackle. Do *not* use a strong, bright fluorescent pink. Use the fly as a top dropper, fishing it slowly back and holding it for several seconds on the 'bob'.

3 New Zulu

Hook: Sizes 10–12–14.
Tying silk: Black.
Tail: Prominent fluorescent lime-green floss.
Body: Black Antron or seal's fur or substitute.
Rib: Silver oval thread.
Hackle: Long-fibred black cock, palmered.
Head: Clear or black varnish.

The normal red-tailed Zulu has been popular for many years, but in recent seasons flies incorporating fluorescent lime-green have had success—the Montana and Viva, for example. So to try a New Zulu with this deadly tail colour was a natural progression.

I have found the New Zulu excellent on a fast-sinking line early in the season. It works well as a top dropper in March, April and May, especially on the big reservoirs. Indeed, it is one of the best flies I know for the 'hang' method in early season, and it has helped me make many big catches in competitions.

4 Doobry

Hook: Sizes 8–10–12.
Tying silk: Black.
Tail: Fluorescent-red wool.
Body: Gold Lurex.
Rib: Fine gold wire.
Hackle: Hot-orange and black hen mixed and palmered.
Head: Clear varnish.

This is a Scottish fly and a favourite of Orkney's top fly-fisher, Stan Headley. It is a good pattern for peaty lochs, where it is easily picked out by the wild browns. I have seen it used on the reservoirs during the last couple of years, and one top angler was trying to keep its success a secret. That speaks for itself!

5 Morey's Claret Palmer

Hook: Size 12.
Tying silk: Red.
Body: A dubbing mix of two parts claret and one part fluorescent-red seal's fur or substitute.
Rib: Silver tinsel.
Hackle: Medium ginger cock, palmered.
Head: Clear varnish.

Once a top fly-fisher at Grafham and elsewhere, Bob Morey gave me two or three of these palmers to try after I had managed to find him some fluorescent-red seal's fur. Unfortunately, Bob started to play a lot of golf, and now we rarely see him at Grafham. However, I will always be grateful to him for this fly, which has brought me great success. Note the slim, sparse body, and use the pattern as top or a middle dropper when you are wondering what to fish there.

6   First C.D.C. Palmer

Hook: Size 10.
Tying silk: Black.
Tail: White Antron clipped short.
Body: Glo-Brite fluorescent-red floss.
Rib: Silver oval thread.
Hackle: Two *cul-de-canard* hackles dyed chestnut-brown and palmered.
Head hackle: White *cul-de-canard*.
Head: Black varnish.

This pattern takes *cul-de-canard* hackle-feathers one step further. They can be bought dyed different colours, so experiment with them. This is my first serious effort at a *cul-de-canard* top dropper. Initial tests indicate that I am on the right lines; it floats well and has a mobile action. Because of the thick stalks of the longer *cul-de-canard* hackle needed for palmering, great care and patience is called for in tying them in.

Fish this pattern as top dropper on a floating line in light to moderate winds. In stronger winds, with a higher wave, it can be fished at any position on the leader.

7   Draycote Sedge

Hook: Sizes 10–12–14.
Tying silk: Orange.
Tail: Fluorescent-orange floss, not overdone.
Body: Dubbed fiery-brown and a few fibres of red seal's fur or substitute.
Rib: Fine silver wire.
Hackle: Honey cock, palmered.
Head hackle: Light ginger cock.
Head: Clear varnish.

This is a good, steady form-book summer pattern which, although it began life at Draycote, has travelled well to many reservoirs and lochs. It comes into its own from early July until the season's end. Fish it, of course, as a top dropper on a floating line.

8   Olive and Honey

Hook: Sizes 10–12.
Tying silk: Olive or black.
Body: Gold Lurex.
Rib: Gold oval thread.
Hackle: Two long-fibred hackles, one honey cock and one olive cock, mixed and palmered.
Head: Clear varnish.

This is another good all-rounder to be used when olives, olive buzzers or olive mayflies are coming off. It was Brian Thomas, of Nottingham, who first sang the praises of this one, and Nick Nicholson regards it as 'one of the best palmer flies for Pitsford reservoir in summer'.

The long-fibred hackles gives this fly extra mobility when it is retrieved through the waves.

Weighted Flies

GOLDHEADS

Roman Moser, the well-known Austrian river fly-fisher has made a video called *New Ways of Fishing the Caddis*. Anyone who has not seen it should try to get a copy. Roman uses many flies in the video, but those that have captured everyone's imagination are the Goldheads. These are nymphs which have drilled gold-plated brass balls for their heads. The ball is slid round the hook-bend and down to the eye, where it is secured with tying silk. Three different sizes of brass ball are used.

---

1   Black Goldhead

Hook: Size 10 with medium gold ball.
Tying silk: Black.
Tail: Black cock hackle-fibre.
Body: Black Antron.
Rib: Silver oval thread.
Hackle: Black hen.
Head: Clear varnish.

A general black nymph is good for much of the time and travels well from water to water. The Black Goldhead is no different, except that it seems to out-perform the others. It can be fished with confidence in rivers, lakes and reservoirs. Fish it on the point with other light flies as droppers.

---

2   Olive Goldhead Nymph

Hook: Sizes 10–12 with medium or small gold ball.
Tying silk: Olive.
Tail: Light-olive cock hackle-fibres.
Body: Medium-olive seal's fur or substitute.
Rib: Fine gold oval thread.
Thorax: Same as body.
Shellback: Cock pheasant tail feather-fibres.
Hackle: One or two turns of light-olive cock.
Head: Clear varnish.

The Olive Goldhead is suitable for rivers where olives hatch for much of the season. It is heavy enough to reach bottom quickly, making it ideal for upstream nymph fishing, a deadly approach when trout or grayling are easily visible in clear, wadeable rivers. Use it on an AFTM 6 floating fly-line, with perhaps a size 16 spider pattern on a dropper two feet up the leader.

3   White Goldhead Tadpole

Hook: Size 10 with medium gold ball.
Tying silk: White.
Tail: Fluorescent-white marabou.
Body: Fluorescent-white chenille.
Shellback: White feather-fibre over gold ball.
Head: Clear varnish.

This is a good, fast-sinking mini-white lure which closely imitates a small fish. The gold ball is said to make it more attractive to trout. I am not sure about this, but I concede that it works well. I tend to prefer it to other white-mini lures, at least for starters.

---

4   Goldhead Shrimp

Hook: Sizes 10–12 with medium or small gold ball.
Tying silk: Olive or black.
Body: A mixture of three parts olive, one part red and one part orange Antron.
Rib: Fine gold oval thread taken completely over shellback.
Hackle: Palmered light-olive hen.
Shellback: A strip of thick, clear plastic.
Head: Clear varnish.

This is an ever-popular weighted nymph for river fly-fishers who try for grayling as well as rainbows or brown trout. As shrimp become more numerous at certain times of season, usually from June to September, and are found more often in trout's stomach, fish it in the 'dead-drift' or 'rolled-nymph' style with a dropper for bonus fish.

---

5   Goldhead Hare's Ear

Hook: Sizes 10–12 with medium or small gold ball.
Tying silk: Brown.
Tail: Hair fibres from hare's ear.
Body: Rubbed hare's ear fur; carrot-shaped.
Rib: Fine gold oval thread.
Thorax: Dubbed hare's ear fur.
Throat hackle: Whisks of hair from hare's ear.
Shellback: Black feather-fibre.
Head: Clear varnish.

Yes, another Hare's Ear variant, but need I say any more? Anyone who fishes regularly knows the merits of any kind of Hare's Ear Nymph, and this is merely another excellent pattern for rivers or stillwaters.

6 Goldhead Pheasant Tail Nymph

Hook: Sizes 10–12 with medium or small gold ball.
Tying silk: Brown.
Tail: Cock pheasant tail feather-fibres.
Body: Cock pheasant tail feather-fibres, carrot-shaped.
Rib: Fine copper wire.
Thorax: Cock pheasant tail feather-fibres.
Throat hackle: Long fibred ginger hen.
Shellback: Cock pheasant-tail feather-fibres.
Head: Clear varnish.

To fish this pattern you need a floating line, a five-metre leader of 3lb breaking-strain, and lots of slow, patient retrieving.

It can be a marvellous pattern when fished on a reservoir in a side wind and the line is allowed to drift round on its own while the fisher merely takes in excess slack. If takes are timid, fit a sight-bob on the end of the fly-line. This is also a good river nymph for trout and grayling.

7 Goldhead Orange Caddis

Hook: Size 10 with medium gold ball.
Tying silk: Black.
Body: Rusty-orange micro-chenille (Veniard).
Wing: A bunch of long fibres from a large ginger cock hackle.
Thorax: Black ostrich herl.
Head: Clear varnish.

I have tried this neat little caddis imitation only recently, but I am told it has a great early form on both rivers and stillwaters. It has accounted for a lot of fish on Welsh waters and on Chew Valley Lake.

8 Goldhead Brown Caddis

Hook: Size 10 with medium gold ball.
Tying silk: Black.
Body: Medium-brown micro-chenille (Veniard).
Wing: A bunch of long fibres from a large ginger cock hackle.
Hackle: Black ostrich herl.
Head: Clear varnish.

Neither this nor the orange version are well known, but Gary Evans tells me this one has good form. I like to think I have a good eye for a new fly even before it sees water, and I have the right 'vibes' about both these patterns.

TINHEADS

The Tinhead hook has without doubt started a new fashion in flies, nymphs and lures. Its predecessor, the Leadhead, in which a lead-shot was pinched on or Super-glued to the hook-shank just behind the eye, was crude by comparison.

Tinheads pose no after-problems. The weight is soldered in place and cannot cast off as split-shot can. Also, the weight's position is such that the nymph always swims upright and on an even keel.

I worked on the hooks with Colin Wilson, but the perfected job was down to him. However, I could see the mount gave great scope for developing a whole range of patterns, both imitative and attractors. My first deadly pattern was a Redhead, but at the same time Jeanette Taylor created a whole range of deadly patterns.

---

1 Red-and-black Tinhead

Hook: Size 10 Tinhead pre-painted with black varnish.
Tying silk: Black or red.
Tail: Red marabou.
Body: Red marabou dubbed on.
Rib: Fine gold oval thread.
Hackle: Palmered honey or white.
Head: Clear varnish over tying-off thread only.

Pitsford regular Dick Underwood swears by this pattern. He says 'it never fails there, even when the fishing is difficult according to other fly-fishers'. He calls it his secret weapon. His great faith in it has prompted me to try it on occasions, and it does seem to be a great all-rounder. It can be exceptionally good fished deep when trout are known to be feeding on bloodworms.

---

2 Jeanette's Damsel Tinhead

Hook: Sizes 8–10 Tinheads pre-painted with yellow eyes with black pupils.
Tying silk: Black or olive.
Tail: Olive marabou.
Body: Olive marabou dubbed on.
Rib: Fine gold oval thread.
Hackle: Palmered light grizzle.
Head: Clear varnish over tying-off thread only.

Jeanette Taylor's Damsel Tinhead is the best known of these patterns. I have never had it fail, and it has caught more double-figure rainbows from small fisheries than any other fly. The Dever Fly Fishers' Club has virtually adopted it as its favourite pattern. I have found it works equally well on Rutland, Pitsford, Ravensthorpe, Grafham, Ringstead and Horseshoe lake. It was even a top fly for me in New Zealand.

Fish it on a floating-line except in very cold conditions in early season, when an intermediate or slow-sinker may work better. It's a fly to pin your faith on!

3 Small-fry Tinhead

Hook: Sizes 8–10 Tinheads pre-painted with yellow eyes with black pupils.
Tying silk: White.
Tail: White marabou; a few strands of pearl Crystal hair are optional.
Body: White marabou dubbed on.
Rib: Fine silver oval thread.
Hackle: Palmered light grizzle or honey.
Head: Clear varnish over tying-off thread only.

This works well as a general pattern, but excels from July onwards when the coarse-fish fry hatch in the weed-beds. At this time I have used the fly from the dam wall at Grafham and caught six fish in a morning session in blazing sun while few others caught anything. All I did was cast out a long line with a WF8 floating line and then allow the Tinhead Fry to sink on a five-metre leader. Now I allow a side light wind to fish the fly round for me while I slowly retrieve slack line. I have mentioned one example, but this is a proven method anywhere where small coarse fish are in a trout fishery.

In New Zealand the pattern imitated the small fish called smelt, and I landed rainbows of 6lb 10oz, 5lb 4oz and 5lb 4oz in less than half-an-hour on Lake Tarawera.

4 Fluorescent-orange Tinhead

Hook: Size 10 Tinhead pre-painted either with yellow eyes and black pupils or with the whole head painted fluorescent orange.
Tying silk: Orange.
Tail: Fluorescent-orange marabou.
Body: Fluorescent-orange marabou dubbed on.
Rib: Fine gold oval thread.
Hackle: Palmered light-grizzle or honey.
Head: Clear varnish over tying-off thread only.

This fly either works like crazy or fails. I have been fortunate enough to do extremely well with it, my largest rainbow going 12½lb and my best brown, 8lb 1oz, which seems to prove that specimen fish are partial to it.

If imitative patterns are not working on any still-water, give this one a try. Floating sink-tip or intermediate lines are recommended with a leader of at least 6lb breaking strain.

5 Fluorescent-pink Tinhead

Hook: Size 10 Tinhead pre-painted with yellow eyes and black pupils.
Tying silk: White.
Tail: Fluorescent-pink marabou.
Body: Fluorescent-pink marabou dubbed on.
Rib: Fine silver oval thread.
Hackle: Palmered grizzle or honey.
Head: Clear varnish over tying-off thread only.

Similar to the orange Tinhead and an out-and-out attractor, this pattern scores well when fished on a sinking line. Make a long cast, allow the lure to sink well down, and then retrieve quite fast with the lure close to the bottom. It is primarily a rainbow-catcher, but a similar small lure tempted a wild brown of 18lb 13½oz for Steve Hunt when he fished Wentwood Reservoir in South Wales. Keep an open mind!

6 Brown Tinhead

Hook: Size 10 Tinhead pre-painted with yellow eyes and black pupils.
Tying silk: Black or brown.
Tail: Brown marabou.
Body: Brown marabou dubbed on.
Rib: Fine gold oval thread.
Hackle: Palmered light grizzle or honey.
Head: Clear varnish over tying-off thread only.

We are back to an imitative pattern with this one. It could represent any of several different food-forms—a leech, a larva, a nymph, a worm, or a fish. After Jeanette's Damsel Tinhead, this has proved the second best in deceiving trout. It produces the best results when fished very slowly on a floating fly line, with length of leader varied according to the depth of the water.

7 Black-and-green Tinhead

Hook: Size 10 Tinhead painted bright fluorescent-green.
Tying silk: Black.
Tail: Black marabou.
Body: Black marabou dubbed on.
Rib: Fine silver oval thread.
Hackle: Palmered light grizzle or honey.
Head: Clear varnish over tying-off thread only.

This pattern is for early season (March, April) or late season (October) and into the now available winter rainbow fishing. I used it a lot in 1991 and 1992, usually with a sinking line—intermediate or slow-sink in mild conditions, but fast-sink when it was very cold. It is now a 'must' in my fly-box.

8 Redhead

Hook: Size 10 Tinhead painted bright red.
Tying silk: Black.
Tail: Black marabou.
Body: Black marabou dubbed on.
Rib: Fine silver oval thread.
Hackle: Palmered light grizzle.
Head: Clear varnish over tying-off thread only.

This was the first pattern I devised and then tried with such devastating results. It worked everywhere, and soon I could catch my day's quota far too early. Obviously I was on to something. I later realized that it was the hook which was the success story, for it allowed superb presentation on a floating line.

TINHEAD DEVELOPMENTS

The idea for these patterns which I developed with Colin Wilson (for the mounts) and Jeanette Taylor (for some superb patterns) is moving on. In this set we have gone for more imitative designs for all types of stillwater and river, with many suitable for both, as I have proved.

The point to remember about all Tinheads is that you must have the imagination to turn the fixed weighted head to your advantage in looks as well as performance. This is done by painting on various eyes, or a dark thorax, or a grub's head, or whatever.

These patterns are always used on the point, either singly or with another lighter or unweighted fly or nymph on the dropper.

---

1 Corwen Nymph

Head: Size 12 Tinhead with the head painted white or yellow.
Tying silk: Black.
Body: Dubbed grey rabbit fur.
Rib: Fine gold wire.
Hackle: A very short length fibred black hen.
Head: Clear varnish.

This pattern was the idea of Mike Green, a bailiff on the Welsh Dee. He decided that a short hackle would fit neatly between the eye and the fixed Tinhead. It was the first time this had been tried, and Mike found the trout and grayling on his Corwen stretch took the nymph better than the normal Hare's Ear variants. The nymph has since been shown to work on many other rivers. It imitates a caddis larva, which is why it is taken so confidently.

---

2 Olive Grub

Hook: Size 10 Tinhead coated with black varnish.
Tying silk: Olive.
Body: Dubbed mix of two parts of olive Antron and one part of grey rabbit fur with a few fibres of orange Antron.
Rib: Gold oval thread.
Head: Clear varnish.

This drab-olive grub will pass for virtually any bottom-crawling insect. It should be fished at small fisheries on a long leader and floating line. It has been particularly successful in the South of England and on Cotswold waters.

3 Tinhead Daddy

Hook: Size 10 Tinhead coated with black varnish.
Tying silk: Brown or black.
Body: Single strand of dull-yellow wool.
Rib: Tying silk.
Legs: Six knotted cock pheasant tail feather-fibres.
Wings: Two cree cock hackle-tips the length of the hook-shank.
Hackle: Red game cock.
Head: Clear varnish.

Trout really do have a passion for eating craneflies or, as we fly fishermen call them, daddy-long-legs. So many 'Daddies' are blown on to the surface of reservoirs in late summer and autumn that trout become used to them. What they do not seem able to do is to spot the difference between a daddy on the surface and one on the bottom. I think this is because the fish recognize daddies as safe food items. Having fished the sunken Tinhead Daddy for more than two seasons, I can say that trout seem more partial to the sunken pattern than to the floater.

4 White-headed Stick

Hook: Size 10 Tinhead coated with white paint.
Tying silk: Black.
Tail: A few strands of pearl Crystal.
Body: Bronze peacock herl.
Head: Clear varnish.

Sedge and caddis larvae are common food items in all rivers and stillwaters, and they have seen many imitations. This is one of the latest. Already I have caught a lot of trout on it in three different countries. It is another nymph to be fished deep and slow.

5 March Brown Tinhead

Hook: Size 10 Tinhead coated with white paint.
Tying silk: Brown.
Body: Medium-brown Antron thickly dubbed.
Rib: Tying silk.
Hackle: Brown partridge.
Head: Clear varnish.

Mainly a river pattern, this one is suited to spate rivers in Scotland, Wales and northern England. It is really a general pattern to be used when you are fishing and moving, searching out new likely looking spots. Brown trout and grayling are the main quarry, but stocked rainbows are easy to tempt with this nymph.

6   Extra Long Tail

Hook: Size 10 Tinhead painted with yellow eyes with black pupils.
Tying silk: Brown.
Tail: Olive marabou four times the length of the hook.
Body: Hare's face hair dubbed on.
Rib: Thin gold oval thread.
Head: Clear varnish.

It was that outstanding small-fishery specialist Peter Cockwill who first realized that a longer-than-normal tail worked better than others in marabou lures. This did not mean only in weighted, leadhead types, but in weightless surface lures as well. The extra wiggle during a rapid twitch retrieve undoubtedly causes many fish to attack the lure. Peter won the Wilcon Classic small-fishery championship at Dever Springs in two successive years with this type of lure.

7   Ultimate Caddis Larva

Hook: Long-shank size 10 Tinhead coated with black varnish.
Tying silk: Olive.
Tail: Yellow wool burned to give black spot at end (grub's head).
Hackle: A rear hackle of grey partridge tied to form feeler legs around the grub's head.
Body: Olive hare's face hair and natural brown mixed to form a dubbing.
Head: Clear varnish.

This is the best Caddis Larva I have devised. The burned wool gives a perfect grub-head imitation. The fly works on rivers, small fisheries and reservoirs, and seems to completely fool the trout, browns and rainbows. Takes are confident and come on a very slow retrieve as the larva trips along the bottom. I have hooked several fish with the nymph lying static on the bottom. The pattern can be used throughout the season. It's a must!

8   Claret Tinhead

Hook: Size 10 Tinhead painted with yellow eyes with black pupils.
Tying silk: Claret.
Tail: Claret marabou.
Body: Claret marabou dubbed on.
Rib: Fine gold oval thread.
Hackle: Palmered honey cock.
Head: Clear varnish.

Popular though claret is in many flies and nymphs, it never seems to be used in marabou patterns. I am a claret fan, so when I found a sample pack of this colour marabou, I set to and tied a half-a-dozen Tinheads. One thing was for sure: no trout, even on hard-fished waters, had ever seen one of these before. It caught as well as any of the other colours.

MINI CAT'S WHISKER LURES

The original Cat's Whisker lure, introduced in the mid-nineteen-eighties, was tied on a size 8 or 6 long-shank hook. It has been a great success at both small fisheries and reservoirs. In early trials it produced a brace of 14lb rainbows for its inventor, David Train. He told me how well it had worked on a number of waters, and I was soon able to confirm that big reservoir trout couldn't resist it. Smaller flies came into fashion as we approached the nineteen-nineties, including unweighted mini-versions of the Cat's Whisker in sizes 12 and 10. They won many competitions, including some championships.

I later experimented with flies in various colour schemes and tied on size 10 hooks, but I kept the weighted bead-chain eyes. It is these I feature in this set.

1 Mini Cat's Whisker

Hook: Sizes 10–12, with a pair of medium weight bead-chain eyes attached.
Tying silk: Black.
Tail: White marabou.
Body: Fluorescent-yellow chenille.
Wing: White marabou.
Head: Clear varnish.

This mini-version of the original was a lucky fly for me when I visited New Zealand in 1991. I stopped alongside a large lake called Rotoma. It was sunny, the water was shallow and gin-clear, and my companions said, 'Don't bother! It's too bright!' I agreed with them, but decided to have a few casts. I was set up with an intermediate fly-line and this mini Cat's Whisker on the point with a Damsel Nymph on a single dropper. After about ten casts I was into a big fish, my first in New Zealand—and more than 6lb. I was very pleased. Yes, it picked out the Cat's Whisker as many thousands of fish have; it's not coincidence any more. I returned the fish after a quick photograph.

2 Mini Black-and-green Cat's Whisker

Hook: Size 10, with a pair of medium weight bead-chain eyes attached.
Tying silk: Black.
Tail: Black marabou.
Body: Fluorescent-green chenille.
Wing: Black marabou.
Head: Clear varnish.

This one has a colour combination which is known as a great attractor. The weighted head is not too severe, just enough to get the lure deep down even on a floating line fished from the bank. Slow and deep is a good tactic with this pattern.

3 Mini Black-and-orange Cat's Whisker

Hook: Size 10, with a pair of medium-weight bead-chain eyes attached.
Tying silk: Black.
Tail: Black marabou.
Body: Fluorescent-orange chenille.
Wing: Black marabou.
Head: Clear varnish.

The first time I tried this fly was on a winter's day at Dever Springs. Nothing much had been happening all morning, and after about ten fly-changes I put on this fly for its baptism. It was an instant success and a four-fish limit for 25lb followed. It is a pattern well worth a try at small fisheries.

4 Mini Orange Cat's Whisker

Hook: Size 10, with a pair of medium-weight bead-chain eyes attached.
Tying silk: Black.
Tail: Fluorescent-orange marabou.
Body: Fluorescent-orange chenille.
Wing: Fluorescent-orange marabou.
Head: Clear varnish.

This is a good all-rounder, and a colour well-known as a rainbow attractor. Fish it by making long casts with a sinking line chosen according to the depth of water. The retrieve should be quite fast, with occasional very fast bursts.

5 Mini Olive Cat's Whisker

Hook: Size 10, with a pair of medium-weight bead-chain eyes attached.
Tying silk: Black.
Tail: Olive marabou.
Body: Olive chenille.
Wing: Olive marabou.
Head: Clear varnish.

Dare I say it? We are back here to a Damsel Nymph look-alike! Whatever the fish take this one to be it fishes well on a really slow retrieve on a floating line. The eyes of all these lures obviously have some attraction, for scientists have told us that trout have a trigger mechanism which reacts to eyes. They say all our lures should have them in one form or another for best results.

6 Mini White-and-red Cat's Whisker

Hook: Size 10, with a pair of medium-weight bead-chain eyes attached.
Tying silk: Black.
Tail: White marabou.
Body: Fluorescent-red chenille.
Wing: White marabou.
Head: Clear varnish.

This could be taken for a small fish. It certainly seems to put a fish or two in the bag in those horrible conditions of coloured water after a big wind has stirred up the water. It fishes best on a sinking line.

7 Mini Black-and-red Cat's Whisker

Hook: Size 10, with a pair of medium bead-chain eyes attached.
Tying silk: Black.
Tail: Black marabou.
Body: Fluorescent-red chenille.
Wing: Black marabou.
Head: Clear varnish.

The colour combination of this pattern has been seen in other successful lures. It is little wonder that it catches its fair share of rainbows and browns. All the lures in this set have that pulsating mobile tail and wing; and the weighted eyes allow for a jig retrieve. Mix these qualities with the various colours to suit conditions, and you have an unbeatable set of lures.

8 Mini Yellow Cat's Whisker

Hook: Size 10, with a pair of medium-weight bead-chain eyes attached.
Tying silk: Black.
Tail: Fluorescent-yellow marabou.
Body: Fluorescent-yellow chenille.
Wing: Fluorescent-yellow marabou.
Head: Clear varnish.

This is another good fly for coloured water, and particularly when the brown stain–like algae is affecting fishing. This 'nasty' appeared at Grafham in 1991 and just would not disperse even though more water was continuously pumped into the reservoir. Most fly-fishers struggled during this period, as the trout just could not see flies that were presented. This one, and the orange, swung the odds a little towards the angler.

HEAVY RIVER BUGS

Heavily weighted river bugs are a necessity for all serious river fly-fishers, but especially for those who fish powerful rivers with white-water rapids flowing into deep pools. This is where the largest trout and grayling lie close to the bottom, and ordinary leaded nymphs sink neither deeply enough nor quickly enough to reach them. The heavier nymphs in this collection sink very quickly even through strong white water, so that by the time one enters a pool, it is close to the bottom and easily seen by the fish. Its speed will be natural for any food item swept into the pool.

A single dropper two feet from the point nymph can be used, and I would advise a small spider pattern. Use a floating line and sight bob for bite indication, and perhaps a weighted braided leader on a floating line.

1 Polish Claret Bug

Hook: Sizes 10–12, curved type, heavily weighted with lead-wire.
Tying silk: White.
Body: Hairy claret wool.
Rib: Copper wire.
Head: Prominent white and clear varnish.

This Claret Bug was shown to me by Adam Sikora, a member of the Polish World Championship Team. He had been catching well in the Championships on the Welsh Dee and I tied a couple to try for myself. After being drawn on a deepish pool, I caught six grayling of good size in three hours on this hard-fished river.

2 Grey Hare Nymph

Hook: Size 10, heavily weighted with lead-wire.
Tying silk: Black.
Tail: Three black pig bristles.
Body: Very dark brown hare's fur from mask.
Rib: Copper wire.
Shellback: Grey partridge hackle-fibres.
Cheeks: Long grey partridge hackle-fibres.
Head: Clear varnish.

Originally tied for two strong-flowing Finnish rivers, Kitka and Kuusinki, this fly accounted for most of more than fifty grayling for me in one session on the Kitka. I have since proved it on rivers as far apart as the Test and the rivers of New Zealand's North Island.

154

3 Rangitaiki Stick Nymph

Hook: Long-shank, size 10. Heavily leaded with lead-wire or bottle-top lead-foil strip.
Tying silk: Black.
Body: Dark-brown Antron.
Rib: Medium gold oval thread.
Thorax: Yellow Antron.
Hackle: Very sparse brown partridge.
Head: Clear varnish.

New Zealand's famous Rangitaiki river was running high and its bottom was a mass of moving pumice stone on the first occasion on which I fished it. Returning two days later, I realized the water would still be well above normal and that a heavy nymph was needed. I decided a caddis grub imitation might work and tied this pattern accordingly. Result: seven good rainbows to 3lb, a most pleasing catch in the conditions. The secret was to keep the nymph working deep along the bottom until it came to rest under my own undercut bank. The nymph has since worked well in weirpools on English rivers.

4 Green Killer Bug

Hook: Size 10, heavily weighted with lead-wire.
Tying silk: Black.
Body: Dubbing mix of olive Antron and hare's ear fur.
Thorax: Dark-green Superla dubbing (seal's fur substitute).
Hackle: Brown partridge.
Head: Clear varnish.

This is an excellent general pattern, again representing a caddis. Lift any moss-covered stone from the river-bed and you will see all sorts of caddis grubs, and many have this coloration. Such a drab little nymph can often cause the downfall of one of a river's old and cunning fish. Specimen fish make only one mistake—unless you are feeling generous and release it.

5 The All-black

Hook: Size 10, heavily leaded with lead-wire to form a carrot-shape.
Tying silk: Black.
Tail: Brown partridge hackle-fibres.
Body: Black Antron or any seal's fur substitute.
Rib: Copper wire.
Shellback: Black feather-fibre.
Head: Clear varnish.

The name implies New Zealand influence, and this is the type of heavy nymph used on their powerful rivers. Black, in lure, dry or nymph as in this case is always a winner. Fish it in a style similar to that used for other heavy nymphs.

6 Olive-and-brown Nymph

Hook: Size 10, heavily leaded with lead-wire to form a carrot-shape.
Tying silk: Black.
Tail: Brown partridge hackle-fibres.
Body: Medium olive-green seal's fur or substitute.
Rib: Copper wire.
Shellback: Dark-brown feather-fibre.
Thorax: Dark-brown seal's fur or substitute.
Head: Clear varnish.

Similar in size, shape and weight to the All-black, this fly shows a change of colour. Try using a black Spider as a dropper with this one. For a further change, try the ever-reliable Red Tag.

7 Red Test

Hook: Sizes 10–12, heavily weighted with lead-wire.
Tying silk: Black.
Body: A mix of grey rabbit body fur and grey Antron.
Rib: Tying silk.
Thorax: Red Antron.
Hackle: Ginger hen.
Head: Clear varnish.

This is a bug I tied for grayling fishing on the Test during November and December. It brought me massive catches on several occasions, with a few fish topping 2lb. This is a very good nymph for winter grayling. Fish it slowly away from fast currents. The nymph shown is one that has caught twenty-two grayling.

8 Nettie Bug

Hook: Sizes 10–12, heavily weighted with lead-wire.
Tying silk: Black.
Body: Medium-brown Antron.
Rib: Gold wire.
Thorax: Light-grey Antron.
Hackle: One turn of brown partridge.
Head: Clear varnish.

A larger version of this was used at small fisheries for recently stocked rainbows, but this is a pattern I decided to try for general river fishing in a bottom-dragging style for wild trout and grayling. It has worked well, bringing good catches of both from rivers such as the Wharfe, Test, Dee and Derwent.

ZONKER LURES

The use of natural and dyed rabbit fur has become fashionable during the last decade. Dubbed fur is good for nymph bodies, while the longer-fibred white fur, or the same dyed black, is excellent for wet-fly wings.

When the American Zonker streamer lures became popular in England in the late nineteen-eighties, at first only natural rabbit fur was used. But white fur was soon being dyed in various colours, and an excellent range was developed.

1 Genies Pink Zonker

Hook: Long-shank, sizes 6–8.
Tying silk: Fluorescent pink/red.
Body and tail: Pearl Mylar piping.
Wing: Rabbit fur dyed washed-out pink. Cut a thin strip complete with skin and attach it at tail and head.
Throat hackle: Bright-pink hackle-fibres.
Head: Clear varnish.

The first time I used this Jeanette Taylor (Genies Flies) lure, I hooked a 7½lb rainbow trout. The pattern has remained a lucky big-trout catcher ever since and seems to work well with stocked large trout at small fisheries. The pink fur comes from Sparton tackle, who dye it to perfection. My best results have come when fishing the lure singly on a 4-metre leader of 6lb breaking strain nylon and a medium-sink line.

2 Original Zonker

Hook: Long-shank, sizes 6–8.
Tying silk: Black.
Body and tail: Silver Mylar piping.
Wing: Natural brown rabbit fur. Cut a thin strip complete with skin and attach it at tail and head with red silk.
Throat hackle: Natural brown rabbit fur.
Head: Black varnish.

Designed as a small fish-imitating lure, the Original is still excellent. On English reservoirs it is in late August, September and early October, when small coarse fish gather in the margins, that this lure is at its best. It has accounted for many big wild trout in recent years—that is browns and rainbows which have grown on from pound stockies to as much as 10lb.

If trout are chasing fry up to the surface, a floating or intermediate line is all that is needed. Sometimes, when extra-long-range casting is needed, a size nine shooting-head might be better. With double-haul casting, you should hit the 40-metre mark.

3 Yellow Zonker

Hook: Long-shank, sizes 6–8.
Tying silk: Red.
Body and tail: Pearl Mylar piping; alternative, silver.
Wing: Rabbit fur dyed yellow. Cut a thin strip complete with skin and attach it at tail and head.
Throat hackle: Grizzle cock fibres.
Head: Clear varnish.

This is a good pattern in murky water, when this colour stands out and is very visible to the trout. In gin-clear water, such a bright colour could scare fish. It is also worth trying at the reservoirs in early season, especially from a boat anchored in deep water.

4 Olive Zonker

Hook: Long-shank, sizes 6–8.
Tying silk: Red.
Body and tail: Pearl Mylar piping.
Wing: Rabbit fur dyed olive. Cut a thin strip complete with skin and attach it at tail and head.
Throat hackle: Grizzle cock fibres.
Head: Clear varnish.

This lure was devised after rabbit fur had been dyed olive as dubbing for various nymphs. It was later used as wings in some wet-fly mini-Zonker patterns. Finally a Zonker lure was tried. I have no experience of this one, but friends say it can be extremely good in the summer when most fly-fishers are pre-occupied with small artificials.

5 Orange Zonker

Hook: Long-shank, sizes 6–8.
Tying silk: Red.
Body and tail: Pearl Mylar piping, alternative gold.
Wing: Rabbit fur dyed orange. Cut a thin strip complete with skin and attach it at tail and head.
Throat hackle: Grizzle cock fibres.
Head: Clear varnish.

This is a good all-round pattern and, like all orange lures, scores in the warm weather of high summer when a fast retrieve is used. It is also good in coloured water—that is reservoir water which normally is clear but has been stirred up by a big wind and carries a milky tinge.

6 *Red Zonker*

Hook: Long-shank, sizes 6–8.
Tying silk: Red.
Body and tail: Pearl Mylar piping; alternative silver.
Wing: Rabbit fur dyed red. Cut a thin strip complete with skin and attach it at tail and head.
Throat hackle: Grizzle cock fibres.
Head: Clear varnish.

Red is not much used when new lure patterns are being designed, but the few red lures I know of are all extremely good on their day. They need to be fished very deep on a fast-sinking line for best results.

---

7 *Black Zonker*

Hook: Long-shank, sizes 6–8.
Tying silk: Red.
Body and tail: Pearl Mylar piping; alternatives silver or gold.
Wing: Rabbit fur dyed or natural black. Cut a thin strip complete with skin and attach it at tail and head.
Throat hackle: Grizzle cock fibres.
Head: Clear varnish.

Black lures of varying shapes and sizes are well-known as great trout-catchers. This modern black lure is another good one to be used in early-season-fishing.

---

8 *White Zonker*

Hook: Long-shank, sizes 6–8.
Tying silk: Red.
Body and tail: Pearl Mylar piping.
Wing: White rabbit fur cut in a thin strip complete with skin and attached at tail and head.
Throat hackle: Grizzle cock fibres.
Head: Clear varnish.

This fish-imitating lure has shown outstanding consistency on the big reservoirs, in particular at Rutland and Grafham, where many specimen fish have fallen to it. Use it on floating and intermediate lines from the bank and medium or on a fast-sinking line from a boat. Use a leader of at least 6lb breaking-strain. If you hook your 'dream fish', you want to make sure you land it!

SMALL FISH-IMITATING LURES

This collection consists of four floating small-fish patterns and four realistic sinking small-fish patterns. Fly-fishers usually refer to the small fish on which trout feed as 'fry'. On the big reservoirs these are usually perch or roach, and they can be newly hatched one-inch-long pin-fry in July up to five- or six-inch yearlings in September. Whichever they are, trout feed on them, and we fly-tyers have had to become almost model-makers in imitating them. I certainly have long specialized in developing various fish-imitating lures.

Catching specimen wild fish from reservoirs and loughs is so satisfying!

1 Yellow-tailed Rainbow

Hook: Long-shank leaded and fish-form shaper, sizes 6–8.
Tying silk: Olive.
Tail: Yellow marabou.
Body: Pearl Mylar stretched tight and painted to look like a mini-rainbow trout—white belly, dark-olive back with black spots, and a red flash down the flank.
Eyes: White with black pupils.
Head: Clear varnish.

We are back to model making, I am afraid, and you will not tie too many of these in half-an-hour. This pattern and the next one were given to me by Micky Bewick, the well-known London fly-fisher.

2 Olive-tailed Rainbow

Hook: Long-shank leaded and fish-form shaper, sizes 6–8.
Tying silk: Olive.
Tail: Olive marabou.
Body: Pearl Mylar stretched tight and painted to look like a mini-rainbow trout—white belly, dark-olive back with black spots, and a red flash down the flank.
Eyes: White with black pupils.
Head: Clear varnish.

This is simply a tail variation from the yellow pattern, but sometimes this can make all the difference. These weighted lures seem to work on all stillwaters—reservoirs, gravel-pits and small lakes. Use them on a floating or slow-sinking line.

3 Sideways-floating Fry

Hook: Extra long-shank nickel Mustad, size 6.
Tying silk: White; use also for underbody.
Tail: Mixed teal feather-fibres and a few strands of pearl Flashabou or pearl Crystal.
Body: White Plastazote shaped like a fish in a sideways position and stuck on. Colour the body with a grey Pantone pen, dark on top of back and gradually paler down the flanks.
Eyes: Painted white; then red with a black pupil.

This is a really clever version of a stunned or dead surface-floating small fish. It is used mostly in late summer and in autumn, when trout on the large stillwaters begin to feed in earnest on the real thing. It is excellent for early-morning or late-evening bank-fishing: just allow the lure to sit on the surface as you would a dry fly and wait for the action!

4 Sinfoil's Pin Fry

Hook: Medium-shank, size 10.
Tying silk: Black.
Underbody: Rear half white silk; front half, fluorescent-red wool.
Overbody: A strip of stretched clear polythene.
Wing: Feather-fibres from silver mallard breast feather.
Head: Black varnish; eyes optional.

Ken Sinfoil invented this lure as a size 6 long-shank twenty years ago. However, only in the last two seasons have I realized how good it is at pin-fry time. It is small enough to be legal in competitions in July. Drift close to the shore, using it as a point-fly on a slow-or medium-sinking line, and you will be sure to see some action!

5 Pearly Pin Fry

Hook: Long-shank, size 12.
Tying silk: White.
Underbody: Fluorescent-red wool.
Tail, back and overbody: Pearl Flashabou.
Eyes: Small pearl plastic beads with black-varnished pupils.
Head: Clear varnish.

Fish this in and around weed-beds in the shallow margins of the reservoirs during July, when newly hatched roach and perch are about and trout home in to feed on them.

6 Pearl Mylar Fish

Hook: Long-shank leaded and fish-form shaper, sizes 4–6.
Tying silk: Black.
Tail: Green pearl Crystal.
Body: Pearl Mylar stretched on tightly; add extra colour to the back with orange Pantone pen.
Eyes: Bright-red with black pupils.
Head: Clear varnish.

This well-weighted, fishy-looking pattern is the product of modern synthetic materials, and it looks the part. I have yet to try it, but I am told it catches well when trout are fry-bashing. It comes highly recommended.

7 Pitcher's Pearl-eyed Fry

Hook: Long-shank, size 6.
Tying silk: White; use also for underbody.
Tail: White marabou.
Body: White Plastazote, shaped and stuck on.
Back and thorax: Fluorescent-yellow chenille.
Eyes: Large white pearl beads.
Head: White Plastazote, shaped and stuck on.

Londoner Geoff Pitcher, the originator of these two lures, was a regular at Queen Mother Reservoir during its peak in the late nineteen-eighties. He gave me twelve of his buoyant lures to try and they have caught quite a few trout for me. The large buoyant pearl-bead eyes give the same effect as in the Booby patterns. Fish this one on a floating or a sinking line, sink-and-rise style.

8 Pitcher's Floating Fry

Hook: Long-shank, size 6.
Tying silk: White; use also for underbody.
Tail: White marabou and pearl Flashabou.
Body: Shaped white Plastazote stuck on.
Gills: Red Ethafoam.

This can be fished similarly to the Sideways-floating Fry on a floating line. It is also good when fished on a fast-sinking line with a shorter leader. The inbuilt buoyancy floats the lure off the bottom while the line remains on it. Retrieve in short, slow twitches to give a sink-and-rise action to the lure.

165

MINI-MUDDLERS

The Muddler Minnow was an overnight success when it arrived in Britain in the late nineteen-sixties. Grafham Water had just opened and was producing unforgettable fishing. Big flies, which we call lures, were 'in'. Anything black, white or orange on a size 6 hook was catching those specimen rainbows and browns. The Muddler, publicized by Tom Saville, soon became the new reservoir fly-fishers' favourite. Its great versatility was that not only was it so buoyant that it floated, but that it could be used also on a fast-sink line. That was a great asset, especially with summer rainbows.

It soon became fashionable to tie Muddlers of varying colours. My pure-white Muddler caught me my then largest brown trout in 1967, 5lb 1oz, taken from the bank. I had first seen this big fish attacking minnow shoals close to the shore.

1 White Mini-Muddler

Hook: Sizes 10–12.
Tying silk: White.
Tail: Fluorescent-yellow floss, alternative, red.
Body: Silver tinsel.
Wing: White swan or goose feather.
Head: Pure-white deerhair clipped cone-shaped. Clear varnish over normal whip-finish.

This is not unlike my original successful pattern, except for the fluorescent-floss tail. This fly quickly tempts any fry-feeding fish that are about, browns or rainbows. Use it on a floating line or, if in deep water a sinker. A fast retrieve usually brings most takes. It is a pattern mainly for reservoirs and gravel-pits.

2 Soldier Palmer Mini-Muddler

Hook: Sizes 10–12.
Tying silk: Black.
Tail: Fluorescent-red floss.
Body: Fluorescent-red floss.
Rib: Fine gold or silver oval thread.
Hackle: Palmered dark ginger to varying shades of brown.
Head: Natural deerhair clipped to ball-shape. Clear varnish over normal whip-finish.

This is a deadly summer surface fly. Use it on a floating line, either as a point-fly with a fast retrieve or as a top dropper with a slower retrieve and finally 'bobbed'. It is definitely a big-water fly, especially for reservoir rainbows in a good wave. Lately, though, it has been found to kill wild browns on the big Scottish, Welsh and Irish waters, even as far north at Orkney. Never go boat-fishing in high summer without trying one. It occasionally works well fished singly and static.

3   Pearl Invicta Mini-Muddler

Hook: Sizes 10–12.
Tying silk: Yellow.
Tail: Golden pheasant crest feather.
Body: Pearl Lurex.
Body hackle: Palmered long-fibred brown cock.
Throat hackle: Jay or blue gallena.
Wing: Hen pheasant tail feather-slips.
Head: Deerhair dyed yellow and clipped ball-shape.
Clear varnish over normal whip-finish.

Flies such as the Invicta and Silver Invicta have been successful general wet patterns for many years, but recently the Pearl Invicta has become popular as a top summer fly when sedges are on the water. It seemed a good idea to turn it into a Muddler by adding a yellow deerhair head.

This fly first proved itself on Chew Valley in August 1991, and it has continued to impress. Fish it on a floating line with a steady, slow retrive.

4   Orange Crystal Mini-Muddler

Hook: Sizes 10–12.
Tying silk: Black.
Tail: Orange Crystal fibres.
Body: Orange floss.
Rib: Medium-silver tinsel.
Wing: Squirrel tail dyed orange and mixed with orange Crystal.
Head: Natural deerhair, half-clipped to give a hackled effect. Clear varnish over normal whip-finish.

Though this is not as bright as the other orange design, it can be fished similarly with good effect. It also works with slower retrieves when used as a top dropper bob-fly. Give it a go on a fast sinker when you are fishing in depths of ten to twelve feet.

5   Fluorescent-orange Mini-Muddler

Hook: Sizes 10–12.
Tying silk: Black.
Tail: Fluorescent-orange floss.
Body: Fluorescent-orange floss.
Rib: Gold oval thread.
Wing: Rabbit fur dyed fluorescent orange.
Head: Natural dark deerhair clipped cone-shape.
Clear varnish over normal whip-finish.

This one is the ultimate fast-stripping mini-lure for high summer and autumn, when rainbows are in the finest condition. Cast it as far as you can on a floating line and then retrieve fast and watch out for following rainbows creating huge bow waves. This is a most exciting, but tiring, way of fishing. It is a proven match-winning fly on English reservoirs.

6 Black Rabbit Mini-Muddler

Hook: Sizes 10–12.
Tying silk: Black.
Tail: Fluorescent-red floss.
Body: Black floss silk.
Rib: Fine silver oval thread.
Wing: Rabbit fur dyed black.
Head: Natural deerhair trimmed cone-shape. Clear varnish over normal whip-finish.

The Black Rabbit is a good early-season fly for bottom-grubbing on a fast-sinking line. Use it from the bank in April, with long casts to allow the line to sink to the bottom before being retrieved with slow-ish, even pull. It will catch in any position on the cast when used in a team.

7 Zulu Mini-Muddler

Hook: Sizes 10–12.
Tying silk: Black.
Tail: Fluorescent-red floss.
Body: Black Antron.
Rib: Fine silver oval thread.
Head: Natural deerhair clipped to ball-shape. Clear varnish over normal whip-finish.

The Zulu is one of the oldest traditional British wet flies, but we have changed it into a Mini-Muddler. Why? It has been found that it works even better in a wave of six inches or more because of the disturbance caused by the Muddler head on the retrieve. Use it as a top dropper with confidence on any boat-fishing session when a floating line is being used. It scores on all waters in Britain and Ireland, and it has travelled well, too, from Spanish and Finnish rivers to Tasmanian lakes.

8 Viva Mini-Muddler

Hook: Sizes 10–12.
Tying silk: Black.
Tail: Fluorescent-green floss silk.
Body: Black Antron.
Rib: Fine silver tinsel.
Wing: Pair of natural black hen hackle-tips.
Throat hackle: Black cock hackle-fibres.
Head: Natural deerhair clipped ball-shaped. Clear varnish over normal whip-finish.

This set of Mini-Muddlers includes several well-known traditional wet flies modified and turned into a new style of fly. As any fly-fisherman on the International match scene will tell you, they are often so deadly that their use can make the difference between winning and losing.

The Viva Muddler is a great all-rounder and I would use it with confidence just about anywhere, from bank or boat, on floating, intermediate or fast-sinking lines, on river or stillwater. It even catches sea-trout in rivers at night.

LARGE LURES FOR LARGE FISH

Some English-reservoir fly-fishers like to try big-fish-or-nothing tactics, particularly at the big two, Rutland and Grafham. Both reservoirs produced a number of double-figure browns in 1992, and they both had their rainbow records broken. At Grafham it happened twice with fish of 11lb 8oz and 13lb 13ozs, while Rutland's best moved up to 11lb 13oz. As these rainbows were stocked at only one pound, they were prestigious fish to catch.

Trying for big fish by design rather than taking pot-luck obviously gives a much better chance of catching one. Most big fish eat large numbers of coarse-fish fry.

---

1   Five-inch Extra-light Tube-fly

Hook: Five inches of light plastic tubing with a size 6 treble fitted when in use.
Tying silk: Red and white.
Body: A sleeve of silver or pearl Mylar tubing, tied in at the rear with red silk and again in the centre and varnished.
Wing: Change to white tying silk and for the upper wing use a spray of pearl Flashabou one inch longer than the body tube. For the lower wing, use a similar amount and length of silver Flashabou.
Head: Build up large white head and cover it with white Tippex; then paint on the eyes.

The great asset of this large, fish-like lure is its lightness, which makes it easy to cast on an AFTM 9 fly-line and suitably powerful rod.

Fish it from an anchored boat over known shoals of small roach, perch or bream, which will mean that a few big trout will also be in attendance. Known hotspots at Rutland have been forty feet deep, with very fast-sinking lines or lead-core shooting-heads needed to get the lure down fast. The South Arm just past the Yacht Club and right in the centre are worth trying. Many big trout have been caught here on such lures.

---

2   Yearling Roach Fly

Hook: A light plastic tube 2½–3-inches long with a size 8 treble fitted when in use.
Tying silk: Red and white.
Body: Slide on a sleeve of silver or pearl Mylar tubing and tie it off with red silk at the rear and centre.
Wing: Change to white tying silk and for the upper and lower wings tie in a mixed spray of four parts of pearl Twinkle to one part of pearl Flashabou; for the top wing, use a small spray of black Flashabou.
Head: Build up large white head, cover it with white Tippex and paint on eyes.

This size tube represents yearling roach, of which millions abound at Grafham and Rutland. Being slightly smaller, it is easier to cast, and I often use an AFTM 8 weight Hi-D fly-line when fishing at depths of up to twenty feet.

Do not forget to fit a small piece of clear plastic tube over the end of the tube-fly to receive the shank of the treble when the hook is tied on and pulled back.

3 Orange-and-yellow Tube

Hook: A 2 or 2½-inch lightweight tube with a size 8 treble fitted when in use.
Tying silk: Red and white.
Body: A sleeve of silver or pearl Mylar tubing slid on and tied at the rear and centre with red tying silk.
Wing: Change to white tying silk and for the upper wing use a mixture of orange Crystal and fine pearl Flashabou; for the lower, yellow Crystal and silver Flashabou.
Head: Build up large white head and cover it with white Tippex; then paint on the eyes.

This is more a fancy and colourful tying, but it still looks like a small fish when in the water. Fish it similarly to the others. This pattern has given me the best results. It is well worth trying.

4 Luminous Tube

Hook: Two ½-inch pieces of clear tubing, one taking a size 6 or 8 treble when in use.
Tying silk: Black.
Body: A tube of Starlight (which activates when bent and is luminous in the dark) fitted into the two tubes.
Wing: Orange Crystal overwing and a pearl Twinkle underwing tied to the front tube piece.
Head: Clear varnish.

This illuminated lure fished on a sinking line seems to catch fish in the deepest, darkest areas of a lake or reservoir. Lots more work needs to be done on it, but sea-fishers have used similar luminous Starlights close to their baits to great effect.

5 Dutch Pike Lure

Hook: A size 2/0 Aberdeen nickel sea-hook in tandem with a size 8 treble attached with 40lb nylon.
Tying silk: Orange.
Wing: Yellow bucktail, white bucktail, pearl Crystal and, at the eye, mauve bucktail, all tied on in little bunches on top of the hook to leave the orange tying silk prominent. Cover the silk with clear Sparkle nail-varnish.
Head: Orange tying silk coated in clear Sparkle nail-varnish.

Catching pike by accident or design on feathered fly lures is good fun. This lure was given to me by Paul Vekemans, who fishes fly in the dykes of Holland. These specialist lures catch a lot of pike, sometimes beating bait and spinner. The feathered lure can be retrieved more slowly than a spinner, allowing the angler to work the weedbed 'ambush areas' better.

6 *Frank's Rubber Duck*

Hook: Size 6 or 8 long-shank threaded on to the white eel-like waggle tail.
Tying silk: White or red.
Hackle: Bright-red; six turns.
Head: Clear varnish.

Frank Cutler showed me this variant of the Waggy. The kits are popular and are on sale in most tackle-shops. They come in all colours. This fly will take a fish or two from deep down when all else fails.

7 *Redgill Waggy*

Hook: Size 2 nickel supplied with Redgill Waggy kit.
Tying silk: White.
Underwing: White marabou topped with double the amount of lime-green.
Overwing: Lime-green Crystal hair.
Eyes: Large jungle-cock feather or substitute.
Head: Clear varnish.

This has given me terrific results at Rutland with better-than-average fish, mostly rainbows. Rutland was where the Waggy lure became famous, and this pattern adds to the collection. It works best stripped very fast, but not necessarily deep.

8 *Crystal-and-Marabou Tandem*

Hook: Two size 6 long-shank hooks joined in tandem with 20lb nylon.
Tying silk: Black.
Tail: Long red cock hackle-fibres.
Body: Silver Mylar tinsel on both hooks.
Underwing: White marabou feather on both hooks.
Overwing: Orange Crystal on both hooks.
Throat hackle: Long red cock hackle-fibres.
Head: Black varnish; eyes are optional.

Tandem lures were all the rage for big fish in the nineteen-seventies, and they had a very good record of positive hooking. This pattern, incorporating fine orange Crystal as an overwing, can be used from the bank or an anchored boat, but is perhaps best fished from a boat drifting bow-first on the rudder, the anglers side-casting, letting out a few metres of slack line to get the depth, and retrieving in a wide semi-circle.

173

STILLWATER LURES

Stillwater lure patterns come and go in phases. Visit any reservoir in the UK early in the season and, as likely as not, nine out of ten fly-fishers will be using a sinking line and lure. This is a fact, whatever the purists would have us believe, so lure patterns cannot be ignored. This collection includes some good killers showing a swing towards olive, a colour now rivalling the old favourites of orange, black and white.

---

1 Olive Pitsford Perch Fry

Hooks: Long-shank, sizes 6–8–10.
Tying silk: White.
Tail: Two-thirds olive marabou and one-third white.
Body: Gold Mylar tube.
Wing: Two-thirds olive marabou and one-third white.
Head: Clear varnish.

This is another Wayne Gibbons lure for Pitsford, where his faith in olive brought excellent results. If everyone had been using this lure, perhaps it would not have been so successful. But now the secret is out!

Wayne took his use of olive further because of the vast numbers of perch fry all around the reservoir's margins and in and around the weed-beds. His new lure started well with big catches from the bank at Brixworth Bay, fish to more than 3lb. Later Wayne was pleased to catch a 6lb 3oz brownie from Pitsford Gorse Bank, the best brown to be caught from the water in more than three years. Since stocking is with fish of less than a pound, this was a prestigious catch.

---

2 Cutler's Tadpole

Hook: Size 10, with a small shot Superglued on shank at the eye.
Tying silk: Olive.
Tail: Olive marabou.
Body: Rubbed olive marabou.
Rib: Gold oval thread.
Hackle: Olive hen, palmered.
Head: Paint the whole head fluorescent lime-green and then, when dry, paint fluorescent-yellow eyes, followed, when dry, by black pupils. Clear varnish over whip-finish.

The painting of lead-headed Tadpole-style flies was begun by Jeanette Taylor with her famous Tin-heads. That experienced old-timer, Frank Cutler, was not slow to pick up the idea and came up with this mini-lure. It is similar to other olive lures, but Frank insists the head coloration and eyes give it the edge. Fish it on a floating or sinking line throughout the season.

3 Gibbon's Perch Fry

Hook: Long-shank sizes 6–8–10.
Tying silk: Black.
Tail: Two-thirds olive marabou and one-third white.
Body: Olive chenille with two turns of white chenille behind the eyes.
Rib: Copper wire.
Eyes: Medium-weight chain-beads.
Head: Clear varnish.

This lure was developed by a young fly-fisher, Wayne Gibbons, with help from his father. Both fish at Ravensthorpe and Pitsford, and this lure was accepted by trout at both waters much more readily than the conventionally coloured designs once the first month of the season had passed, with lots of fish to 4lb caught from the bank. Then, in October 1991, young Wayne showed all the top rods the way when he won the Pitsford Bank Competition with fourteen fish, his closest rival taking only six fish. All fell to this lure fished on a slow-sinking line.

4 Red Fish

Hook: Long-shank, sizes 8–10.
Tying silk: White.
Tail: White marabou.
Body: Pearl Mylar tubing.
Wing: White marabou, topped with phosphorescent-yellow Flashabou.
Head: Undercoat with white Tippex and finish with fluorescent-red paint. Clear varnish the whip-finish.

This red-headed fish-lure has caught some fine trout, including rainbows to more than 6lb and browns to more than 5lb, all on fast-sinking lines with the lure retrieved along the reservoir bed. I recommend this one from personal experience.

5 Mini-Vulturine

Hook: Size 10.
Tying silk: Black.
Body: Silver tinsel.
Wing: Pair of vulturine guinea-fowl special feathers.
Head: Clear varnish.

This mini-lure uses vulturine guinea fowl feathers with their unique markings. Twenty-five years ago Dave Steuart gave me a big lure on a size 6 long-shank hook which incorporated these feathers. I believe it was called an Elver Lure. It was an impressive lure that caught fish from the bank at Grafham. This small version, which I have tried when mini-fry are about in July and August, is one for the future.

6 Skinny Green Eye

Hook: Sizes 8–10, with medium chain-bead eyes.
Tying silk: Black.
Tail: Sparse white marabou.
Body: Black ostrich herl.
Rib: Silver oval thread.
Eyes: Painted lime-green.
Head: Clear varnish.

This pattern was given to me in France by a continental fly-fisher fishing in the European Championships. He told me it had been his top pattern for two seasons. The secret, he said, was that it must be fished as you would a nymph, with a slow figure-of-eight retrieve on a floating line.

7 Furzer's Hanningfield Lure

Hook: Long-shank, sizes 4–6.
Tying silk: Black.
Tail: White marabou topped by dark-green Twinkle which is left over-length to form the back.
Body: Slide on a tube of pre-drilled white Plastazote.
Thorax: Deerhair dyed orange and clipped very close.
Back: Pull down the dark-green Twinkle to complete the back.
Eyes: Two pearl beads.
Head: Clear varnish.

Brian Furzer regularly fishes at Hanningfield, in Essex. In 1992 the reservoir produced nearly twenty double-figure rainbows of between 10lb and 12lb. The favoured method was to fish a buoyant fly or lure on a fast-sinking fly line and a one-metre leader. Yes, the Booby-nymph method has moved on to 'fishy' type lures as well. Good one, Brian!

8 Green-and-black Leadhead

Hook: Size 10, with medium lead-shot Superglued close to the eye.
Tying silk: Black.
Tail: Black marabou.
Body: Fluorescent lime-green chenille.
Hackle: Green cock, palmered.
Eyes: Yellow with black pupils.
Head: Black varnish.

This mini-Leadhead lure has those deadly Viva colours of lime-green and black. The quite heavy lead-shot glued in at the head makes it sink much faster than any other lure. I have had tremendous results with it at many different waters. In France, at Lac de la Landie, I had twenty trout on it, topped by a 7lb 6oz steelhead on it. Fish it on a long leader on a floating or intermediate line and retrieve it in a series of twitches.

MINI-ZONKERS

Mini-Zonkers are such effective little lures because they have wings of rabbit fur in bunches rather than on the skin. This makes a highly mobile wing which many feel beats even marabou. Certainly the squid-like motion seems irresistible to all kinds of trout in all kinds of water when the fly is retrieved with a slow, pause, slow technique.

Of the various colour matches some work best in stocked rainbow lakes and reservoirs, while others are good for wild browns in lochs and rivers.

This selection of eight contains a basic idea which, with imagination, you can carry further. The flies were devised by Jeanette Taylor from Northampton.

---

1 Black-and-green Mini-Zonker

Hook: Medium-shank, size 10.
Tying silk: Black.
Tail: Fluorescent lime-green floss.
Body: Silver Bobbydazzlelure.
Throat hackle: Fluorescent lime-green hackle-fibres.
Wing: Bunch of black rabbit fur.
Head: Black varnish.

With characteristics similar to those of the deadly Viva, this lure can be even deadlier. It fishes well on all sinking lines at the big reservoirs and is definitely one to try.

---

2 White-and-pink Mini-Zonker

Hook: Medium-shank, size 10.
Tying silk: Black.
Tail: Fluorescent-pink floss.
Body: Silver or pearl Bobbydazzlelure.
Throat hackle: Fluorescent-red hackle-fibres.
Wing: Bunch of white rabbit fur.
Head: Black varnish.

The fluorescent pink seems to be a helpful attractor in this good small-fish pattern. It is good in early season on medium-sinking lines from the bank or on fast-sinking lines from an anchored boat. It has produced tremendous catches at Rutland Water.

3 Natural-and-yellow Mini-Zonker

Hook: Medium-shank, size 10.
Tying silk: Black.
Tail: Fluorescent-yellow floss.
Body: Gold Bobbydazzlelure.
Throat hackle: Fluorescent-yellow hackle-fibres.
Wing: Natural brown rabbit fur.
Head: Black varnish.

The Natural-and-Yellow has been used for 'pulling' tactics at the reservoirs, when a lure is cast on a floating line and pulled back through the waves. My idea would be to fish it from a drifting boat and in a fair wind from mid-summer to autumn.

4 Black-and-pink Mini-Zonker

Hook: Medium-shank, size 10.
Tying silk: Black.
Tail: Fluorescent-pink floss.
Body: Gold Bobbydazzlelure.
Throat hackle: Fluorescent-pink hackle-fibres.
Wing: Black rabbit fur.
Head: Black varnish.

I remember trying this pattern for the first time at Hanningfield during an important competition. I used a medium-sinking line with this fly on the point. Result: six fish on a difficult day and I qualified for the English National. Since then I have always tried this particular Mini-Zonker when I have needed some quick fish at any reservoir. It has rarely let me down.

5 White-and-orange Mini-Zonker

Hook: Medium-shank, size 10.
Tying silk: Black.
Tail: Fluorescent-orange floss.
Body: Pearl Bobbydazzlelure.
Throat hackle: Fluorescent-orange hackle-fibres.
Wing: White rabbit fur.
Head: Black varnish.

This one works well in July at most large reservoirs and gravel-pits when newly hatched coarse-fish fry are active in the shallows and around weed-beds. A versatile pattern, it can be fished in any position on a three-fly cast. I tuck it away as a middle dropper, where it picks up many 'bonus' fish.

6 Natural-and-red Mini-Zonker

Hook: Medium-shank, size 10.
Tying silk: Black.
Tail: Fluorescent-red floss.
Body: Silver Bobbydazzlelure.
Throat hackle: Fluorescent-red hackle-fibres.
Wing: Natural brown rabbit fur.
Head: Black varnish.

Similar to the old and successful Butcher, this fly was a sure winner from its first outing. It works in a whole series of fishing styles and weather conditions. An attractor pattern, it works for browns as well as rainbows.

7 Black-and-red Mini-Zonker

Hook: Medium-shank, size 10.
Tying silk: Black.
Tail: Fluorescent-red floss.
Body: Gold Bobbydazzlelure.
Throat hackle: Fluorescent-red hackle-fibres.
Wing: Black rabbit fur.
Head: Black varnish.

This is the most sober fly in the series and one I like to fish on or close to the bottom. It is very good in early season for both rainbows and browns. It has a good catch-record at Grafham.

8 White-and-green Mini-Zonker

Hook: Medium-shank, size 10.
Tying silk: Black.
Tail: Fluorescent lime-green floss.
Body: Silver or pearl Bobbydazzlelure.
Throat hackle: Fluorescent lime-green hackle-fibres.
Wing: White rabbit fur.
Head: Black varnish.

This is again a known killing colour-combination. I recommend that you treat this series as a set of flies which you can chop and change and fish in different styles until you find the one which is best for your water.

Stillwater Nymphs

DAMSEL FLIES

The damsel is without doubt one of the most important summer flies to hatch on most stillwaters. It belongs to the sub-order Zygoptera, and the adults can be distinguished from dragonflies by their much finer bodies. Trout are spoiled for choice of food as the water temperature rises in late June/early July, and it is then that the damsel becomes more and more active and its nymphs form a major part of the trout's diet.

1 Green Bead-eyed Damsel Nymph

Hook: Long-shank, sizes 8–10.
Tying silk: Black or olive.
Tail: Light-olive marabou, kept short.
Body: Dubbed light-olive marabou.
Rib: Fine hackle-stalk.
Thorax: Medium-olive Antron.
Shellback: Brown feather-fibre.
Legs: Brown partridge hackle-fibres.
Eyes: Pair of small green beads.
Head: Clear varnish.

Emerging damsels leave the safety of the weedbeds and then swim quite quickly to the margin or a protruding reed stem. They then crawl from the water and rest briefly before their skins split and they emerge as adults. It is a good idea to try to copy this swimming action when this and other damsel nymph patterns are being fished.

2 Swimming Damsel

Hook: Long-shank, size 8; swimming nymph design.
Tying silk: Olive.
Tail: Dark-olive marabou kept short.
Body: Light-olive mohair.
Rib: Copper wire.
Thorax: Light-olive mohair.
Shellback: Olive Raffene.
Wing-cases: Olive Raffene.
Throat hackle: Dark-olive hen.
Eyes: Chain beads painted black; pupils left silver.
Head: Clear varnish.

The shape of this damsel nymph (which I found in a New Zealand tackle-shop), is much like that of a swimming nymph. It works well enough on British trout to be included in my set of top patterns. It rarely fouls the weeds when fished along the bottom in shallow water because of its upturned eye. This is a valuable asset.

3 Distressed Damsel

Hook: Medium-shank, size 10.
Tying silk: Olive.
Tail: Two-inch long plume of medium- to dark-olive marabou.
Body: Dubbed mix of seal's fur or substitute: 50 per cent medium-olive, 30 per cent golden-olive, 10 per cent light-blue and 10 per cent fluorescent-orange.
Thorax: Same as body.
Wing-pad: Olive raffia clipped to shape.
Hackle: Grey partridge hackle dyed golden-olive. Tie this in on top of the thorax by tip, concave side uppermost then secured down before wing pad.
Eyes: Pearl or red beads secured by a strand of powergum, singed to create pupils and to seal the end.

This is a Charles Jardine pattern. The extra long tail gives an enticing and realistic wiggle. Fish it on a floating fly line when nymphs are hatching.

---

4 Dark Diving Damsel

Hook: Long-shank, sizes 8–10; weighted with lead-wire at head.
Tying silk: Black.
Tail: Pair of light-olive goose biots.
Body: Dark-brown Antron tied carrot-shaped.
Rib: Olive floss pulled tight.
Hackle: Brown partridge.
Head: Bronze peacock herl with clear varnish over normal whip-finish.

This nymph dives quickly, which makes it very effective as a small-fishery special. Trout in the clear waters of south-of-England fisheries are easily seen swimming close to the bottom. A good tactic is to cast well ahead of a slowly cruising fish, allow the nymph to sink into the fish's vision, and then, with a clever retrieve, entice it to take. The dark fly is easily observed in the water, so the take can be seen and the perfect strike made.

---

5 Rabbit Damsel

Hook: Medium-shank, size 10.
Tying silk: Olive.
Tail: Thin strip of light-olive rabbit fur on skin, ribbed with olive tying silk with the end left bushy.
Body: Olive seal's fur or substitute.
Rib: Silver Lurex tinsel.
Hackle: Sparse strands of French partridge.
Shellback: Brown feather-fibre.
Eyes: Red beads joined with red power gum through centre of eyes; singed at ends.
Head: Clear varnish.

This is one of my favourite patterns, again from Charles Jardine. I did very well with it at Grafham the first time I tried it, in July 1990, and since then it has never let me down when damsels have been on the water. Fish it on a floating line.

6 Ethafoam Adult Damsel

Hook: Long-shank, size 8.
Tying silk: Black.
Tail and body: A 4-inch strip of bright blue Etha-foam doubled and then whipped every eighth-of-an-inch, with head section open for further tying.
Wings: Two sprays of natural deerhair from be-neath the thorax; split, then whip down.
Eyes: Thick clear nylon singed at ends.
Head: Completed shellback style, keeping the eyes intact and with clear varnish over a normal whip-finish.

Both rainbows and brown trout do take the adult damsel well from July until the end of August. This is a good unsinkable pattern which is nearer model-making than fly-tying, but do make a few for next summer. Pairs of damsels locked together in mating sometimes briefly drop on to the water and are taken by a trout. Use this pattern when you see this hap-pening.

7 Brown Damsel

Hook: Long-shank, sizes 8–10.
Tying silk: Black.
Tail: Brown marabou.
Body: Brown Antron.
Thorax: Brown Antron; make prominent.
Hackle: Medium-brown hen fibres.
Wing-cases: Brown feather-fibre.
Shellback: Brown feather-fibre.
Eyes: Red beads secured with clear nylon singed at ends.
Head: Clear varnish.

This should be fished similarly to the other weight-less patterns described. A simple colour change can sometimes mean the difference between success and failure. I tend to try this pattern when the more normal olive damsels are not 'producing'.

8 Bob's '92 Damsel

Hook: Long-shank, size 8, weighted generously with lead wire.
Tying silk: Black or olive.
Tail: Golden-olive marabou and bottle-green Spectraflash strands mixed.
Body: Olive chenille.
Rib: Green copper wire.
Thorax: Dubbed *cul-de-canard* feather-fibres dyed golden olive.
Shellback: Brown feather-fibre.
Throat hackle: Pearl Spectraflash strands.
Hackle: Partridge dyed olive; full circular.
Head: Clear varnish.

New materials tend slightly to alter accepted tyings, and this is what happened when I devised a special Damsel nymph. I wanted to imitate the nymph active on the bottom, before hatching, and I decided to add a few attractor high-spots. The pattern was a resounding success.

Fish this weighted nymph slow and deep on a 15ft leader and floating line. As a hatch begins, and sport hots up, I revert to the unweighted surface patterns in this set.

BOOBIES AND SUSPENDER BUZZERS

The Booby Nymph came from Gordon Fraser, who fishes at Eyebrook, and the style of fishing it was an overnight 'smash-hit' with many anglers. Soon the nymphs were being tied bigger and brighter, and some became floating mini-lures. The polystyrene or Plastazote balls which give buoyancy are trapped into a piece of white nylon taken from ladies' tights. Once tied in at the head, these eyes, or 'boobies' as they are known to British fly-fishers, are quite secure.

Although Boobies float, they are fished on fast-sinking lines with varying lengths of leader. The fly-line sinks but the Booby floats up on its leader.

---

1 Black Booby

Hook: Size 10.
Tying silk: Black.
Tail: Black marabou.
Body: Black Antron.
Rib: Medium oval silver thread.
Booby Eyes: Plastazote dyed primrose yellow.
Head: Clear varnish.

The Black Booby was very successful in May 1991, especially at Grafham. The method was to cast as far as possible with a fast-sink line, pause for about ten seconds, and then begin a jerky retrieve. It did best in waters 10 to 12 feet deep.

---

2 Orange Booby

Hook: Size 10.
Tying silk: Black.
Tail: Orange marabou.
Body: Dubbed orange marabou.
Rib: Medium gold oval thread.
Booby Eyes: Polystyrene balls with black pupils.
Head: Clear varnish.

The Orange Booby is purely an attractor pattern, yet amazingly, it fishes well when retrieved very slowly. Orange lures or wet flies normally need a fast retrieve to make them work effectively. This one is the exception.

3 Fluorescent-pink Booby

Hook: Size 10.
Tying silk: Pink or white.
Tail: Fluorescent-pink marabou.
Body: Dubbed fluorescent-pink marabou.
Rib: Medium oval silver thread.
Booby Eyes: Polystyrene balls with black pupils.
Head: Clear varnish.

I remember Brian Leadbetter using the Pink Booby with incredible effect during one of the early European Open Championships at Bewl Bridge. The fishing was not easy in the clear water, and Brian had blanked in the morning boat-fishing session. It was all change to the bank in the afternoon, and I remember struggling hard for two rainbows, hich was a good performance, as most were blanking. But 300 metres along the bank, Brian landed six rainbows and was easily top bank rod. Fortunately for me, I had caught five in the morning from the boat, which gave me third place overall.

4 Brown Booby Nymph

Hook: Size 10.
Tying silk: Black.
Tail: Brown marabou slightly longer.
Body: Dark-brown Antron.
Rib: Fine silver oval thread.
Booby eyes: Polystyrene balls.
Head: Clear varnish.

The Brown Booby is more of a nymph or larva type of fly. It could pass for a leech or a worm. This colour catches more brown trout than the others, except perhaps the white. Fish it in the same style as the others.

5 White Booby

Hook: Sizes 8–10.
Tying silk: Black or white.
Tail: White marabou, longish.
Body: White Antron.
Rib: Silver oval thread.
Booby Eyes: Polystyrene balls.
Head: Clear varnish.

The White Booby must seem like a small fish to the trout, and since small fish are a major food-form it works well. This is my favourite. Fish it in the same way as the others.

6 Black Para Buzzer

Hook: Sizes 10–12.
Tying silk: Black.
Tail: White Glo-Brite floss tied round bend.
Body: Dubbed black marabou or seal's fur or substitute; kept fine.
Rib: Fine silver tinsel; Lurex.
Thorax: Mixed black and brown seal's fur or substitute.
Shellback: Grey feather-fibre.
Wing: Pair of grizzle cock hackle-tips.
Hackle: Top-quality cock grizzle tied Parachute-style round base of ball.
Head: Polystyrene ball trapped in fine nylon from ladies' tights. Clear varnish over normal whip-finish.

Peter Pike's Parachute-hackled Suspender Buzzers were so good that they were on the 'secret list' back in the 1988 and 1989 seasons. I kept quiet about them as they really were deadly. They are fished as dry flies, either on the point of a three-fly cast or occasionally as a top dropper in a high wave. They are excellent for all stillwaters from May until September.

7 Olive Para Buzzer

Hook: Sizes 10–12.
Tying silk: Black.
Tail: White Glo-Brite floss tied round bend.
Body: Dubbed olive marabou or seal's fur or substitute; kept fine.
Rib: Single strand of green Flashabou.
Thorax: Dark-olive seal's fur or substitute.
Shellback: Light-brown feather-fibre.
Wing: Pair of slim grizzle-cock hackle-tips.
Hackle: Top-quality grizzle cock tied Parachute-style round base of ball.
Head: Polystyrene ball trapped in fine nylon from tights with clear varnish over normal whip-finish.

This Olive Para Buzzer has caught some big fish for me on Grafham Water during sparse hatches of a largish olive chironomid in May and June.

8 Orange Para Buzzer

Hook: Sizes 10–12.
Tying silk: Orange.
Tail: White Glo-Brite floss tied round bend.
Body: Dubbed orange marabou or seal's fur or substitute; kept fine.
Rib: Fine silver tinsel; Lurex.
Thorax: Rusty-orange seal's fur or substitute.
Shellback: Light-brown feather-fibre.
Wing: Pair of slim brown cock hackle-tips.
Hackle: Top-quality ginger cock tied Parachute-style round base of ball.
Head: Polystyrene ball trapped in fine nylon from tights. Clear varnish over normal whip-finish.

Try fishing this one on the point and retrieving it against the wave; or if large ginger buzzers are hatching, fish it as a static dry fly.

EMERGING AND ASCENDING CHIRONOMIDS

Chironomids or, as most UK fly-fishers nickname them, 'buzzers' are the trout's most common food in most English reservoirs and large lakes, so it is important that their various stages are well imitated. Emerging or ascending nymphs seem to hold a special attraction for feeding trout, probably because they are such easy targets.

These insects begin to hatch in good numbers by April and continue on and off throughout the season. A dull, cloudy, but mild day following light rain seems to induce large hatches, and the fishing is always good provided you have the right flies on.

1 Olive Glass Buzzer

Hook: Sizes 12–14; lightweight curved type.
Tying silk: Black or olive.
Body: Antron dyed olive-green and tied well round curve.
Rib: Olive Nymph Glass fairly tight but allowing particles of Antron to show through.
Thorax: A small amount of red Antron; then apply wing-cases (*see* below) and finish prominently with dark peacock herl.
Wing-cases: Two slips of tough, clear plastic.
Breather: A snip of plucked white marabou.
Head: Clear varnish.

Many flies that hatch during early summer and through to autumn have an olive coloration, so this is an important fly on all stillwaters. It has often been top fly on a cast of three for me, especially on big gravel-pit fisheries. Fish it in the top few inches with a slow retrieve and on a light floating line.

2 Black Glass Buzzer

Hook: Sizes 12–14; lightweight curved type.
Tying silk: Black.
Body: Black Antron tied well round bend.
Rib: Black Nymph Glass, fairly tight.
Thorax: A small amount of red Antron; then apply wing-cases (*see* below) and finish prominently with dark peacock herl.
Wing-cases: Two strips of tough, clear plastic.
Breather: A snip of plucked white marabou.
Head: Clear varnish.

I often fish this effective pattern in the centre of a three-nymph cast and about six inches down, with a buoyant Suspender Buzzer on the point and, obviously, a floating line. Being a sinker, the Black Glass Buzzer sags the leader just those few inches below the surface, putting it at prime taking depth. Fish it very slow or static.

3 Red Glass Buzzer

Hook: Sizes 12–14; lightweight curved type.
Tying silk: Black.
Body: Bright-red Antron tied well round bend.
Rib: Bright-red Nymph Glass, fairly tight.
Thorax: A small amount of red Antron; then apply wing-cases (*see* below) and finish prominently with dark peacock herl.
Wing-cases: Two strips of tough, clear plastic.
Breather: A snip of plucked white marabou.
Head: Clear varnish.

The red coloration provides two attraction points. Red is the colour of many of the chironomid families' larval stages, and all chironomids show a prominent blood-red colour as they emerge. This one can be fished deeper on the point after the cast has sunk a little.

4 Grey Glass Buzzer

Hook: Sizes 12–14; lightweight curved type.
Tying silk: Black.
Body: Grey Antron tied well round bend.
Rib: Clear Nymph Glass, fairly tight.
Thorax: A small amount of red Antron; then apply wing-cases (*see* below) and finish prominently with dark peacock herl.
Wing-cases: Two strips of tough, clear plastic.
Breather: A snip of plucked white marabou.
Head: Clear varnish.

After these early buzzers have become air-borne and then settled, their body colour often appears to be dark grey. This pattern has that exact appearance, although it must be remembered that the aquatic coloration of this insect is often different from that of the winged adult. But adult flies, with their 'new' colours, are also taken by trout.

5 Peter Pike's Orange Buzzer

Hook: Sizes 12–14.
Tying silk: Orange.
Tail: A few fibres of white polypropylene tied well round hook-bend.
Body: Goose shoulder feather-fibre dyed orange.
Rib: Fine silver oval thread.
Thorax: Fur from hare's mask dyed rust-colour.
Shellback: Greyish/off-white feather-fibre.
Breather: White polypropylene.
Head: Clear varnish.

That immaculate tyer, Peter Pike, sent me this Orange Buzzer, with others in green and black. They all catch fish, but it is with this orange version that I have done so well. Fish it close to or on the surface on a light floating line.

6 Red Emerger

Hook: Sizes 12–14; lightweight curved type.
Tying silk: Black.
Body: Bright-red mohair, wound on.
Rib: Stripped peacock-quill feather-stalk.
Wing: Two white cock hackle-tips.
Thorax: Red dubbing with a little pink mixed in; seal's fur or substitute.
Hackle: Light-ginger hen.
Shellback: Bright-red mohair.
Head: Clear varnish.

It was Bob Carnill who introduced this type of nymph. This one is included because of the importance of the red colour at emergence. The thorax is deliberately large to emphasize the appearance of red, pumped-up blood. It fishes well either static or with an inch-by-inch retrieve. Watch out for fast pluck takes, which are easily missed.

7 Cutler's Midge

Hook: Sizes 12–14.
Tying silk: Black.
Tail: Three or four strands of cock pheasant tail feather-fibres.
Body: Bronze peacock herl.
Rib: Fine gold thread.
Hackle: Sparse honey hen, palmered.
Head: Black varnish.

Frank Cutler has more experience of stillwater trout fishing than any other man I know. At seventy-four he has seen all the new ideas come and go. He will tell you that dry-fly fishing on the reservoirs was once a joke. Anyone using such tactics was looked upon as an eccentric idiot. Like the rest of us, he now knows better and has adjusted to the new thinking. This is one of his midge patterns, which is fished static or very slowly on a light floating line.

8 Midday Midge

Hook: Sizes 12–14.
Tying silk: Brown.
Body: Light-brown natural hare's mask fur; tapered carrot-shape.
Rib: Brown tying silk.
Hackle: Dark-brown cock (known as red game).
Wing: A few strands of white deerhair.
Head: Clear varnish.

This is a general pattern which also fits perfectly into the current dry-midge trend. Because it is rather drab, it passes for any hatching nymph. It is very good fished static in a big wave.

MORE CHIRONOMIDS

Any regular stillwater fly-fisher could devote a whole fly-box to chironomid larvae, pupae and adults. Pupae are found most of all in trout stomach contents, and sometimes, in spring or early summer, a trout's stomach will be packed to capacity, mainly with pupae, but with some larvae as well. Then, in mid- and late-summer, all sorts of food—such as sedges, damsels, corixae snails, shrimps, terrestrials, fry—will appear, but always with chironomid pupae also present. Larger trout may have their stomachs bulging with roach or perch fry, but always a few chironomid pupae will be mixed in among them. Clearly, trout, rainbows or browns, are likely to take an artificial chironomid or buzzer pupae at any time during the season.

---

1 M.P. Buzzer

Hook: Sizes 10–12.
Tying silk: Black.
Body: Pheasant tail feather-fibres dyed black.
Rib: Copper wire.
Thorax: Clear shrink-tubing used for connecting fly-line leaders.
Hackle: Soft, fluffy-white hen; one turn only.
Head: Clear varnish.

This nymph was sent to me by Michael Polin, from Lurgan, Northern Ireland. Michael was so successful with it with the wild brown trout in the loughs that one evening he took fish of 5lb 6oz, 4lb 2oz and 3lb 12oz. To fool quality wild fish such as these needs something special, and I believe this is what we have in Michael's buzzer.

He always fishes the fly on its own on a partially greased leader. Fish rising to take emerging nymphs fall for this pattern every time.

---

2 O.P. Emerger

Hook: Sizes 12–14; curved grub hooks.
Tying silk: Black.
Body: Medium-olive floss.
Rib: Closely tied pearl Lurex.
Thorax: Grey fur from hare's mask.
Hackle: Two turns of light Greenwell's hen.
Shellback: Brown Twinkle fibres.
Head: Clear varnish.

The O.P. Emerger should be fished delicately in the surface film when olive buzzers are hatching. On many stillwaters this is usually from May. It will also take fish when olives are hatching—but don't confuse the two!

3 Smallest Midge

Hook: Sizes 18–20–22.
Tying silk: Black micro.
Body: Black tying silk.
Thorax: One strand of thin bronze peacock herl.
Wing-cases: Grey delicate feather-fibres.
Head: Clear varnish.

This is a pattern for those infuriating occasions when trout are pre-occupied on the tiniest of chironomids. Old fly-fishers used to call it 'smutting', and gave up fishing until the feeding cycle passed. With today's modern tackle, we can fish fine enough without being broken, so tiny patterns such as this are worth keeping in your fly-box.

4 Slim Midge

Hook: Long-shank, sizes 12–14.
Tying silk: Black.
Body: Black tying silk.
Rib: Fine oval copper thread.
Thorax: Grey rabbit's fur.
Hackle: One turn of ginger cock.
Head: Clear varnish.

This very good pattern was passed on to me by Peter Dobbs after he had won two big competitions with it in consecutive weeks at Grafham Water in late May. Conditions were the opposite to what you might think, with a high wave on both occasions. But rainbows can pick out the smallest flies no matter what the wave height—a point worth remembering. Fish it very slow, almost static, on a floating line.

5 Rutland Emerger

Hook: Sizes 12–14; curved grub hooks.
Tying silk: Light olive.
Body: Light-olive floss.
Rib: 3lb breaking-strain clear nylon over whole of shellback.
Shellback: Full-length yellow Raffene before ribbing.
Thorax: Olive Antron and hare's ear fur mixed.
Hackle: Two turns of honey hen.
Head: Clear varnish.

This Martin Blakestone emerging pattern was tied for the difficult bigger fish which live in Rutland Water's South Arm shallows. Martin found olive buzzers and pond olives hatching during similar periods of late May and June, and then again in September. This was a nymph he devised, and it did very well, not only for Martin but for all those of us to whom he passed on the pattern.

6   Lapsley's Bloodworm

Hook: Size 12. Pinch on a small shot at eye and Superglue; or use a Tinhead hook.
Tying silk: Red.
Tail: Bright-red marabou.
Body: Dubbed red Antron.
Rib: Pearl Lurex.
Head: Painted red with clear varnish over.

This pattern from Peter Lapsley imitates a chironomid larva, or bloodworm. Fish it as a point-fly on a long leader from the bank; or on a sinking line from a boat, preferably at anchor. It has produced very good results for me and for my son, Stephen, at Chew Valley—including perch of 3lb!

7   Martin's Apple Green

Hook: Size 12.
Tying silk: Black.
Body: Apple-green floss.
Rib: Fine oval copper thread.
Thorax: Apple-green Antron or seal's fur or substitute.
Shellback: Cock pheasant tail feather-fibre.
Head: Clear varnish.

This is another Martin Blakestone pattern, again developed at Rutland Water, which seems to have more than its fair share of olive or green chironomids. The pattern has worked well for me as a middle dropper on days when occasional fish have been rising. Fish it on a floating, sink-tip or intermediate fly-line according to the day's brightness.

8   Black Latex Midge

Hook: Long-shank, size 12, with small gold-plated brass ball slid on and secured.
Tying silk: Black.
Tail: Black cock hackle-fibres.
Body: A strip of black latex.
Thorax: Black Antron.
Shellback: Black latex.
Head: Clear varnish.

This nymph was given to me by a Dutch fly-fisher who said it was his most deadly pattern on stillwaters. I have found it best when fished from the bank as a point-fly. It has tempted some good fish at small fisheries late in the day after the stockies have been caught.

LONGSHANK GLASS NYMPHS

Nymph Glass is a material to which I was introduced by Gary Evans, and I have rated it very highly ever since I first tried it as a body rib. Because it comes in so many colours, a whole variety of nymphs can be given that life-like, segmented appearance. This useful set of nymphs is suitable for all stillwater trout fisheries, both small and reservoirs.

Nymph Glass is best as a rib over a rough Antron or seal's fur or substitute underbody. Apply it in tight turns, leaving just small gaps where the Antron can poke through. This gives the nymph life and a completely natural appearance.

---

1   Brown Glass Nymph

Hook: Long-shank sizes 8–10 with optional lead-wire weighting.
Tying silk: Brown.
Tail: Two brown goose biots.
Body: Brown Antron tied carrot-shaped.
Rib: Brown Nymph Glass.
Shellback: Black feather-fibre.
Thorax: Brown Antron.
Hackle: Ginger cock.
Head: Clear varnish.

This is a superb point-fly fished slow and deep, and it imitates many different bottom-crawling larvae. Fish it on a floating fly and add a dropper or two of smaller nymphs to maximize your chances.

---

2   Black Glass Nymph

Hook: Long-shank sizes 8–10 with optional lead-wire weighting.
Tying silk: Black.
Tail: Two black goose biots.
Body: Black Antron tied carrot-shaped.
Rib: Black Nymph Glass.
Shellback: Black feather-fibre.
Thorax: Black Antron.
Cheeks: Two black goose biots, one each side.
Hackle: Brown partridge.
Head: Clear varnish.

Fish the Black Glass Nymph in the same way as the brown version and in the main summer months. It is a good early-season pattern as well, especially for anyone wishing to get away from lures. It can be cast well out on a sinking shooting-head and retrieved slowly along the bottom.

3 Red Glass Nymph

Hook: Long-shank sizes 8–10 with optional lead-wire weighting.
Tying silk: Red.
Tail: Cock hackle fibres dyed red.
Body: Red Antron tied carrot-shaped.
Rib: Red Nymph Glass.
Shellback: Claret feather-fibres.
Thorax: Red Antron.
Hackle: Ginger cock.
Head: Clear varnish.

The Red Glass Nymph fishes well at deep-water marks and along dam walls. Fish it on a fast-sinking glass line to achieve long-range casting and the right sinking speed. Takes are felt on the pull with this method.

4 Orange Glass Nymph

Hook: Long-shank sizes 8–10 with optional lead-wire weighting.
Tying silk: Orange.
Tail: Two rusty-orange goose biots.
Body: Orange Antron tied carrot-shaped.
Rib: Orange Nymph Glass.
Shellback: Rusty-orange feather-fibre.
Thorax: Rusty-orange Antron.
Cheeks: Two orange goose biots, one each side.
Hackle: Light-brown partridge.
Head: Clear varnish.

This all-rounder can be fished on all lines and at all depths. It is not as bright an orange nymph as some, but rainbows in particular seem to go for it. I would fish it with confidence on any new water.

5 Dark-olive Glass Nymph

Hook: Long-shank sizes 8–10 with optional lead-wire weighting.
Tying silk: Dark olive.
Tail: Two dark-olive goose biots.
Body: Dark-olive Antron tied carrot-shaped.
Rib: Dark-olive Nymph Glass.
Shellback: Dark-olive feather-fibres.
Thorax: Dark-olive Antron.
Hackle: Medium-olive cock.
Head: Clear varnish.

This is one more effective pattern to add to your collection of olive nymphs, flies and lures. It imitates a damsel nymph quite well, but I use it as a general pattern. Fish it on a floating line. It can be useful on rivers.

6 Light-olive Glass Nymph

Hook: Long-shank sizes 8–10 with optional lead-wire weighting.
Tying silk: Light olive.
Tail: Two yellow goose biots.
Body: Light-olive Antron tied carrot-shaped.
Rib: Light-olive Nymph Glass.
Shellback: Cock pheasant tail feather-fibres.
Thorax: Light-olive Antron.
Hackle: Light Greenwell's hen.
Head: Clear varnish.

This is similar to the Dark-olive, but sometimes, when the trout are choosy, all that is needed is a slight change of colour, or hook-size to have them taking again. Often it is the fly-fisher who keeps changing flies until he finds the killing pattern of the day who comes out on top.

7 Mayfly Glass Nymph

Hook: Long-shank sizes 8–10 with optional lead wire weighting.
Tying silk: Cream or white.
Tail: Cock pheasant tail feather-fibres, with a length of clear Nymph Glass tied in for full-length shellback.
Body: Rear ¼-inch, red Antron; rest, cream or beige Antron pulled down the back and secured.
Rib: 4lb breaking-strain clear nylon.
Shellback: Dark-brown feather-fibre over thorax only.
Thorax: Cream or beige Antron.
Cheeks: Three cream goose biots down each side.
Head: Clear varnish.

Many stillwaters in England as well as rivers have big hatches of mayfly, and the small fisheries of the South and the Cotswolds are the types of waters on which to try this most effective Mayfly Nymph. Chris Ogborne commented when I fished with him at Dever Springs that it was the best new pattern he had seen. Fish it on a floating line and long leader.

8 Yellow Glass Nymph

Hook: Long-shank sizes 8–10 with optional lead-wire weighting.
Tying silk: Black.
Tail: Two yellow goose biots.
Body: Yellow Antron tied carrot-shaped.
Rib: Clear Nymph Glass.
Shellback: Dark-brown feather-fibre.
Thorax: Yellow Antron.
Cheeks: Two yellow goose biots, one each side.
Hackle: Cock pheasant tail feather-fibres.
Head: Black varnish.

This pattern would also pass as a yellow mayfly nymph, but perhaps even better as a caddis. It completes the set of large nymphs that everyone is talking about. Again, fish this one on a floating line and long leader with a slow retrieve.

General Stillwater Collections

BRENIG FLIES (WALES)

Llyn Brenig lies high on the bleak Denbighshire Moors, surrounded by heather and pine forest. It may not be the most fertile of lakes, but at 920 acres it is a large stretch of water. My memories of it are all happy. It was here that I made my International debut in 1984; then again when I became England Captain in 1990.

---

1 Bibio Variant

Hook: Sizes 10–12.
Tying silk: Black.
Tail: Fluorescent-green Glo-Brite floss.
Body: Rear, black Antron, red Antron in centre, and black again for the front section.
Rib: Fine silver oval thread.
Hackle: Black cock.
Head: Clear varnish.

The standard Bibio, which is intended to represent the heather fly, has worked well for many years. At Brenig the addition of the tail blob of fluorescent green makes it an even better fly. The fluorescent highlight works also on other flies, perhaps because of the presence of green leaf weevils. Fish the Bibio on or close to the surface on mild days when a good breeze is blowing.

---

2 Heather Fly

Hook: Sizes 10–12
Tying silk: Black.
Body: Black Antron.
Rib: Black tying silk.
Wing: White feather-fibres.
Legs: Six from knotted cock pheasant tail feather-fibres dyed red.
Head: Clear varnish.

Good numbers of red-legged heather flies can be expected to be blown on to the surface of any lake surrounded by heather.

I have seen good numbers on Brenig, but they occur on many Scottish lochs and Irish loughs as well. The pattern should be fished dry and static.

3   Green Weevil Nymph

Hook: Sizes 12–14.
Tying silk: Black.
Body: Fluorescent lime-green marabou dubbed on.
Rib: Fine silver wire.
Shellback: Fluorescent lime-green Sparton wool.
Hackle: Fluorescent lime-green hackle-fibres; throat only.
Head: Clear varnish.

The green leaf weevil (*Phyllobius viridearis*) is about 5.5mm long and is covered in tiny metallic-like green scales. It lives and feeds in the spruce which grow almost to the water's edge and it appears in large numbers from May to August.

Spooned trout have shown that the fish regularly feed on the insect, so it is well worth imitating its nymphal form. This is the pattern I devised. It deserves a try in summer at Brenig or any other heavily wooded lake.

4   Hal-a-Gwynt

Hook: Sizes 12–14.
Tying silk: Black.
Tag: Gold Lurex tinsel.
Body: Bronze peacock herl.
Rib: Fine copper wire.
Wing: Grey feather-fibre slip.
Hackle: Cock pheasant neck hackle.
Head: Clear varnish.

Known in English as the Sun-and-Wind fly, this is one of the most popular patterns used by Brenig regulars. Fished back through the wave-tops it could represent almost anything. Fish it on a floating line on or close to the surface.

5   Christmas Tree (Mini)

Hook: Size 10.
Tying silk: Black.
Tail: Fluorescent-red Glo-Brite floss.
Body: Black chenille.
Rib: Medium-silver oval thread.
Hackle: Black cock fibres; throat only.
Wing: Black marabou.
Overwing: A fluorescent-green highlight of Glo-Brite floss.
Head: Clear varnish.

This is a killing mini-lure when fished on a fast-sinking line over reasonably shallow water (up to twelve feet). It is very good early and late season, and although it is a winner at Brenig, it works well on all large reservoirs. I once caught thirteen good rainbows on it at Draycote to win a prestigious competition. Originally it was a large-lure design, fished at Rutland on size 6 hooks and even in tandem.

6   Concoction Muddler

Hook: Sizes 10–12.
Tying silk: Black.
Body: Rear end, olive Antron; front half, red Antron.
Rib: Fine gold oval thread.
Hackle: Palmered ginger cock.
Wing: Natural deerhair.
Head: Natural deerhair trimmed ball-shape. Clear varnish.

This fly is a must for the top dropper in warm, cloudy conditions with a good wind. I have known it take four good rainbows in such conditions in half-an-hour on Brenig when others were struggling for a take. It is occasionally fished on the point and retrieved fast. It is normally fished on a floating line, but also 'produces' on a fast-sinking line.

7   Brenig Midge

Hook: Sizes 12–14.
Tying silk: Red.
Tail: Badger cock hackle-fibres.
Body: Stripped peacock quill.
Rib: Red tying silk.
Hackle: Badger cock.
Head: Red varnish.

Lots of the smaller chironomids which hatch on Brenig are not always seen on the more fertile reservoirs of England, and this pattern, given to me by David Griffiths, from Wrexham, has done well. A simple, sparse dressing, it fishes best delicately presented on a light leader and will tempt difficult rising fish.

8   Large Red Sedge

Hook: Sizes 10–12.
Tying silk: Black.
Body: Brown seal's-fur or substitute.
Hackle: Medium-brown cock.
Wing: Brown feather-fibre slips.
Head: Clear varnish.

Not many waters host this larger sedge fly, but Brenig does, with good hatches into the dusk when conditions are right in July and August.

MID-NORTHANTS FLY FISHERS' SELECTION

My good friend Peter Dobbs is a staunch member of the Mid-Northants fly-tying section. The group meets weekly under the masterful eye of Cyril Lineham, who presides over new ideas and new materials and judges the latest inventions. His experience is vast.

The flies, nymphs and lures in this collection are one-off favourites from club members, and each pattern has a proven record. It was Peter who persuaded members of this strong club to pass on these secret favourites.

---

1 Satsuma Sparkler

Hook: Sizes 10–12, up-eyed.
Tying silk: Black.
Tail: Mixed white and hot-orange cock hackle-fibres plus two strands of bronze Crystal.
Body: Bronze Crystal.
Body hackle: Palmered hot-orange and snow-white cock hackles.
Head: Clear varnish.

This pattern was designed by Julian Davies, a local fishing-tackle dealer and keen competition fly-fisher. Fishing in a competition with Peter, he confided that if a few fish were up, he always used this pattern as a top-dropper wake fly, as it could pull fish from yards away.

It is important to use hot-orange and snow-white cock hackles, wound on together. The fly can be fished fast or slow on a floating line.

---

2 Big Foot (snail)

Hook: Sizes 10–12.
Tying silk: Black.
Body: Bronze peacock herl rope formed into a rounded shape.
Shellback: A strip cut from a yellow Ethafoam block.
Head: Clear varnish.

This is a Peter Dobbs pattern for when trout are crunching snails, which occurs from time to time throughout a reservoir season. The fly represents a snail floating upside down with only a vague yellow outline of its foot showing. It should be fished static apart from wind drift. Takes are long, slow draws. You really are dry-fly fishing with this one, so the fly must be treated with flotant.

3 Shwartza

Hook: Size 12.
Tying silk: Black.
Body: Black floss.
Rib: Silver wire.
Wing: Soft black hair, rabbit or squirrel, mixed with a few strands of bronze Crystal.
Head: Clear varnish.

This rather simple fly was devised by Chad Jeyes, but it is perhaps his best. Fish it on the point or as the middle dropper. Peter didn't think much of it at first, but his opinion changed after he caught sixteen trout on it in six hours' fishing at Pitsford.

The wing must be kept short, with no hackle, and the sparse tying must go right round the hook-bend. Fish it on a floating line with a figure-of-eight retrieve.

4 Twitchit

Hook: Size 10.
Tying silk: Black.
Tail: Orange Crystal.
Body: Claret wool.
Rib: Fine oval silver thread.
Body hackle: Claret cock.
Wing: A few long strands of deerhair dyed brownish-orange.
Head: Deerhair as wing, tied in as a bonnet, with clear varnish over a normal whip-finish.

Peter 'discovered' this fly at Pitsford after a bank angler had asked to join him in his boat. A few 'daddies' (cranefly) were on the water, but Peter's normal Daddy pattern was ignored while the Mk 1 version of this fly scored.

Peter worked on the fly and feels the scruffy deerhair bonnet-type head is important, spraying out a little water when it is twitched in the retrieve. The fly should be cast downwind as far as possible, for it is easily seen at distance, even in a big wave. Sometimes it works well if left static, but Peter's favourite retrieve is little twitch pulls with a few seconds' pause between them.

5 Tickerfly

Hook: Sizes 8–10–12.
Tying silk: Black.
Tail: White marabou pinched short.
Body: Silver tinsel.
Rib: Fine silver wire.
Body hackle: Long-fibred grizzle cock.
Head: Fluorescent ball orange chenille, with clear varnish over a normal whip-finish.

Peter tells me an amusing story about this pattern. Ticker Dickens left his fly-box behind after an evening session and the rest of the class opened it up only to find every fly was of the same pattern, but in three hook-sizes.

They had discovered Ticker's 'secret' fly, and naturally assumed that it must be pretty effective if he took the trouble to tie 200 of the same pattern. They returned the box the following week and he revealed all, saying: 'I might not be the best fly-tyer in the class, but I bet this is the most killing fly!'

Of course, everyone tied some, and, yes, it was as good as Ticker said. It is a great all-round pattern on a sinking line in cold conditions and in smaller sizes on a floating line in warm weather.

6 Cyril's Sedge

Hook: Size 12.
Tying silk: Brown.
Body: Dubbed fiery-brown seal's fur or substitute to form a carrot-shaped body.
Rib: Fine silver wire.
Hackle: One turn of long-fibred, medium-brown hen.
Head: Natural deerhair clipped short, with clear varnish over a normal whip-finish.

This is one of the many patterns Cyril Lineham has to his credit. (Another is Cyril's Victor, a great variation of the Invicta.) This little Muddler sedge is at its best in July and August, when it will fool the occasional big, old, wise brown trout. Use it on a floating line, either by itself (when it is most effective) or in a well-spaced team.

7 Cartland

Hook: Long-shank size 10.
Tying silk: Black.
Tail: Fluorescent-pink wool.
Body: Black Antron.
Rib: Fine silver oval thread.
Eyes: Small chain beads.
Head: Clear varnish.

The Cartland is named from the colour of its tail. It should be fished as a point fly about two feet below the surface on a floating or intermediate line. The secret is to fish it slowly as you would a nymph. It was first used at Pitsford, but was afterwards found to work on all the big reservoirs.

8 Dobbie's Olive Nymph

Hook: Long-shank, sizes 8–10.
Tying silk: Dark olive.
Tail: Partridge hackle-fibres dyed olive-green.
Body: Mixed olive and ordinary hare's-ear fur dubbed on.
Rib: Fine gold oval thread.
Shellback: Cock pheasant tail feather-fibres.
Thorax: Pale-yellow Antron or ostrich.
Throat hackle: Partridge hackle-fibres dyed olive-green.
Head: Clear varnish.

Peter Dobbs tells me that this pattern has replaced all his normal Pheasant Tail nymphs in these sizes. Alternated with a normal Pheasant Tail for half-hour periods, Dobbie's proved eighty per cent better. A few close friends have proved its form over six years. My life will be hell for a while when they see this! Ah well! That's the price of progress.

A great method is to fish a three-fly cast with the Twitchit as top dropper, the Shwartza in the centre, and Dobbie's Olive Nymph on the point. On a floating line, with a slow twitch retrieve, you simply cannot fail!

209

STILLWATER FLIES

This selection is a mixture of floating and sinking flies for fishing all kinds of stillwater, from small trout pools to large reservoirs and loughs. Lots of different artificial grasshopper patterns have been devised over the years, the reason being that the 'dapped' natural grasshopper provides probably the deadliest way of taking a wild brown trout off the top on any Irish lough. The New Grasshopper pattern looks the part and has a deerhair tail and body which makes it almost unsinkable.

The two Concrete Bowl mini-lures have shown outstanding form in catching reservoir rainbows in competitions, while the Montana and its variants have become as popular as any pattern in the UK.

---

1 Concrete Bowl (original)

Hook: Size 10.
Tying silk: Black.
Tail: Black marabou, kept short.
Body: Fluorescent-green chenille.
Rib: Fine silver wire.
Hackle: Black hen, palmered.
Thorax: Fluorescent-green chenille.
Head: Clear varnish.

This is the original Concrete Bowl pattern which was named after its early successes at waters such as Toft Newton, with their concrete surrounds, which nevertheless give very good fishing.

I first tried the pattern in a competition at Grafham on a cold May day, when I cleaned up, beating my partner twelve to nil! Fish it on a fast-sinking line in water from six feet to fifteen feet deep.

---

2 Concrete Bowl (Mk 2)

Hook: Size 10.
Tying silk: Black.
Tail: Black marabou, kept short.
Body: Black chenille.
Rib: Fine silver wire.
Hackle: Black hen, palmered.
Thorax: Fluorescent-orange chenille.
Head: Clear varnish.

This pattern is similar to the original Concrete Bowl and works well at all reservoirs, especially from the beginning of April until mid-June. It is of less use from then until the season's end in October. A fast-sinking-line style is again the best method. Use the Mk 2 in conjunction with the original, varying their positions on the leader.

3   Toffee-paper Wickham's

Hook: Sizes 10–12.
Tying silk: Black.
Tail: A few ginger cock hackle-fibres.
Body: Metallic-green tinsel.
Rib: Fine gold wire.
Hackle: Ginger cock, palmered.
Head: Clear varnish.

What a sensational fly this can be on the reservoirs! It was given to me by John Snelson, who had tied the body from metallic-green silver paper taken from a famous brand of chocolate toffee, and I tried it out for the first time in a competition at Draycote. I was seven to one down to top international Tony Curtis until I tied on a Toffee-paper Wickham's. Twenty minutes later it was seven each! The pattern has been responsible for some very good catches on Rutland, and John Eilden won the 100-entry Masterline Challenge with it.

4   Montana Nymph

Hook: Sizes 8–10–12–14; weight optional.
Tying silk: Black.
Tail: Black cock hackle-fibres.
Body: Black chenille.
Hackle: Black hen, palmered through thorax.
Thorax: Fluorescent-yellow or green chenille.
Head: Clear varnish.

The Montana Nymph is probably represented in every fly-fisher's box, because it does, without doubt, catch a lot of trout at small fisheries, where underbody weighted versions are favourite. Smaller unweighted versions on size 12 or 14 hooks are a better choice for the reservoirs. Many colour combinations exist in this immensely popular nymph, so experiment with your own tying.

5   Brown-and-yellow Montana

Hook: Long-shank sizes 8–10, lightly weighted.
Tying silk: Black.
Tail: Brown cock hackle-fibres.
Body: Brown chenille.
Hackle: Brown hen, palmered through thorax.
Shellback: Brown feather-fibre.
Thorax: Fluorescent-yellow chenille.
Head: Clear varnish.

This is the sedge, or caddis-larva, version of the Montana, and it shows how the colour combination can be varied. Fish it on a floating line with a long leader. Droppers can be added to imitate other insects according to the time of year.

6 New Grasshopper

Hook: Long-shank size 8.
Tying silk: Yellow. This fly is tied from the head.
Head: Form a deerhair ball-head by tying a bunch of deerhair all around the hook-shank; then pull back and secure. Clear varnish over normal whip-finish.
Antennae: Two stalks from a brown feather.
Body and tail: Deerhair continued and then whipped into a tube for the tail.
Legs: Two brown hackles with fibres trimmed back to one-sixteenth of an inch from the stalk. Knot the stalks halfway down before attaching them.
Wing: A single cock pheasant back feather.

Given a good wind, a fair wave of one to two feet, an overcast sky and this pattern and you have the ingredients of a memorable day's boat-fishing. Fish the fly as a single on a four-metre leader on a light floating line, and try to keep it static. Better still, use a 15ft dapping rod and a blow-line with a 3ft leader. It is not only on the Irish loughs that this method works. Try it on any big water.

7 Ethafoam Corixa

Hook: Size 12, curved style.
Tying silk: Brown. Then tie in a strip of white Ethafoam and on top of that a strip of brown Raffene. Leave both hanging.
Body: Pearl Lurex.
Rib: Fine silver oval thread ribbed over Ethafoam, which is pulled tight.
Shellback: Complete the back by pulling the brown Raffene tight.
Paddles: Brown goose biots; one each side.
Head: Clear varnish.

This buoyant Corixa should be fished from the bank on a sinking line. Corixae live in shallow water in and around weed-beds. So why fish a sinking line? Because such a line, coupled with a two-foot leader, allows the buoyant Corixa to float off the bottom. A retrieve of a series of regular six-inch twitches gives a sink-and-rise action, similar to that of the natural. Trout often go on corixae eating binges, so this is an important improvement to the pattern.

8 Fidget

Hook: Sizes 10–12.
Tying silk: Black.
Tail: Fluorescent-red floss.
Body: Deep-red seal's fur or Antron.
Rib: Pearl Lurex.
Hackle: Light ginger cock.
Head: A piece of white Ethafoam strip cut to form a round head and two V-shaped points which lie evenly on top of the hook-shank, with clear varnish over a normal whip-finish.

This pattern came from John Hatherall, who fishes Bewl Bridge regularly. He wanted to give the traditional Soldier Palmer more action when it was retrieved across the surface. He achieved his aim with the buoyant head, which makes the fly behave rather like a Muddler when it is pulled fast.

213

INDEX